REWRITABLE
Optical Storage Technology

REWRITABLE Optical Storage Technology

Edited by Judith Paris Roth

Meckler
Westport • London

Library of Congress Cataloging-in-Publication Data

Rewritable optical storage technology / edited by Judith Paris Roth
p. cm.
Includes bibliographical references and index.
ISBN 0-88736-534-5 : $
1. Optical storage devices. 2. Optical disks. I. Roth, Judith Paris.
TA1635.R48 1991
621.39 ' 767--dc20 90-20396
CIP

British Library Cataloguing in Publication Data available.

Meckler Publishing, the publishing division of Meckler Corporation,
11 Ferry Lane West, Westport, CT 06880.
Meckler Ltd., Grosvenor Gardens House, Grosvenor Gardens,
London SW1W 0BS, U.K.

Printed on acid free paper.
Printed and bound in the United States of America.

Contents

Preface

Within two years of the introduction of rewritable optical disk drives by Sony Corporation, there are over fifty announced rewritable optical disk-based subsystems including jukebox products available. Moreover, these products and subsystems are being used extensively for CAD/CAE, medical, pharmaceutical, financial, document management, utilities, remote sensing data, petroleum, applications, Landsat image storage, electronic publishing, and prepress. It is being used as a LAN file server as well as for online database management, data transportability, and backup.

Rewritable optical disk products include Hewlett Packard's Optical Disk Library System, a Direct Access Secondary Storage (DASS) product for both mini- and microcomputer users who require quickly online access to very large quantities of stored information. DuPont is offering FasTrax™, rewritable optical disk-based engineering drawings and documentation management system.

Cygnet and other jukebox manufacturers now offer the possibility of multiple online erasable optical disks. There are rewritable optical subsystems available for Macintosh, OS/2, Xenix, MS-DOS, VAX/VMS, and other platforms.

The objective of this book is to accurately inform the reader about the basics of rewritable optical storage technology and how it can be creatively used for information storage and retrieval. Keep in mind that rewritable optical disk is the latest optical storage technology in a rapidly changing field. This book offers presentations of several university-based applications, an overview of currently available hardware, subsystem and software products and systems, and a technical description of flexible rewritable optical media developed by Optical Data, Inc. and being commercialized by Teijin, Ltd.

Organization of this Book

This book assumes the reader has some grounding in optical storage but is relatively new to rewritable optical storage. It is intended for the potential end-user of a system interested using rewritable optical storage as a primary or secondary storage device. The terms "rewritable" and "erasable" are used interchangeably throughout this book. In addition, erasability refers to the ability to *intentionally* delete data sectors rather than accidental erasure or editing.

Rewritable Optical Storage Technology is divided into the following chapters:

Chapter One, "Overview of Rewritable Optical Disk Storage" includes brief descriptions of magneto-optical, phase-change and dye polymer rewritable optical media as well as several new approaches. In addition, it discusses the basic characteristics of rewritable storage, standards, and a look at the emerging market and application trends. An annotated directory of companies and organizations working with rewritable optical storage products is provided.

Chapter Two, "Rewriting the Future: Rewritable Optical Mass Storage Comes of Age" by Robert B. Mueller, Vice President and General Manager of Rewritable Optical Products Division at Sony Corporation of America, focuses solely on magneto-optical rewritable optical disk and its potential impact on the communications and information industries.

Chapter Three, "Software Considerations for Rewritable and Multifunction Optical Drives," written by an experienced optical disk software engineer, provides readers with a basic introduction to the critical points concerning file management software for both rewritable and multifunction optical storage.

Chapter Four, "Development of a Flexible Rewritable Optical Storage Medium" provides the reader an in-depth examination of the complexities of developing a flexible rewritable optical media. Currently under development for commercialization by Teijin, Ltd., this medium was originally developed by Optical Data, Inc.

Chapter Five, "End-User Requirements for Networking an Integrated Rewritable Workstation into a Professional Work Group" was written by an experienced system analyst. This chapter addresses readers who are the end-users for these products and what are their requirements and applications. It examines the dynamics and requirements of work group computing and how they conform with the applications for workstations utilizing rewritable optical storage. This chapter examines some specific applications and explores both the integration of standalone workstations and the development of networked systems using rewritable optical storage to address the requirements

Chapter Six, "Integrated Rewritable Optical Storage Workstations: An End-User's Perspective," the author discusses the uses of optical rewritable media in the development of the Brown, Dartmouth, Harvard Language Workstation Project. Potential applications are discussed in the areas of reference, personalizing reference documents, storage for texts, high-resolution graphics, and sound files. The possible utilization of rewritable optical storage in the humanities with special reference to the areas of foreign/second language instruction is also presented.

Chapter Seven, "Surrogate Manipulation: Early Experiences with the NeXT Computer in a University Research Environment," explains how the University of Iowa has been an early experimenter and adopter of optical storage technology. The University first began experimenting with videodisc technology for the storage of art images in 1981.

In April 1989, the National Endowment for the Humanities sponsored a conference to address problems with cataloging and distributing information about contemporary art collections. As an outgrowth of this meeting, the Computer-Assisted Instruction (CAI) Lab at the University of Iowa is developing a prototype of a computer-based environment that contains the traditional bibliographic information used by librarians, scholarly information known by curators and desired by art historians as well as surrogate manipulative capabilities of use to students and casual users.

At the end of this book is a list of recommended readings as well as a technical glossary of terms and acronyms.

Mention of any company, product, or service does not imply endorsement. Discussion of a product or company does not imply its superiority over competing applications, products, or systems. The errors, inaccuracies, and mis-statements contained in this book are those of the authors.

It is difficult, if not impossible, to publish a book about a dynamic technology, especially when technological breakthroughs, new product announcements and applications are the rule rather than the exception. It is hoped that this book will help the reader become aware of the strengths and limitations of rewritable optical storage and develop a knowledge base to help make informed decisions about its development and use in our information society. It is expected that readers will consider this slim volume the beginning of an ongoing educational and evaluative process concerning rewritable optical storage technology, markets, and application developments.

Judith Paris Roth

List of Trademarks

Trademark	Company
Macintosh	Apple Computers
MCA, PS/2, OS/2	IBM Corporation
Xenix, MS-DOS, PC-DOS	Microsoft Corporation
Unix	AT&T Bell Laboratories
NeXTStep, Mach	NeXT, Inc.
DirectOptical	Jasmine, Inc.
Century Media	Sony Corporation of America
HP-UX	Hewlett-Packard Company
FastTrax	E.I. Nemours DuPont Company
VAX/VMS, Unibus, Q-bus	Digital Equipment Corporation (DEC)
THOR-CD	Tandy Corporation
ETOM	Optex Corporation
Sun, SunOs	Sun Microsystems
LaserDisc	Pioneer Corporation of America
Digital Paper	ICI Imagedata
Ethernet	Xerox Corporation

1
Overview of Rewritable Optical Disk Storage

Judith Paris Roth

This introductory chapter provides a brief overview of rewritable optical storage, a description of rewritable optical disk media, and a comparison of drives. In addition, it presents a discussion of rewritable optical storage characteristics and benefits as well as barriers to its acceptance. In addition, this chapter will briefly consider the competition with other optical information formats — CD and WORM — as well as fixed disk magnetic storage. Lastly, various current and potential application areas of rewritable optical disk will be presented. This chapter provides the reader with an annotated directory of companies and organizations involved with the development of rewritable optical storage.

Benefits of Rewritable Optical Storage

Introduced in 1988 after years of intensive research and development efforts throughout the world, rewritable optical storage offers the computer and communications industry a viable, durable, reliable online mass storage device for workstations, "plug-and-play" subsystems, PCs, mini- and mainframe computers. It is being used as primary and secondary mass storage with standalone and multi-user networks offering advantages over magnetic storage for historical archival storage, unattended backup/storage, and document storage and retrieval methods.

Overall, benefits of magneto-optical (M-O) rewritable storage may be summarized as follows:

- Absence of head crashes
- Removability and compactness
- Reliability: non-contact recording and playback
- Durability: environmentally stable/long archival life
- Conforms to draft ISO/ANSI standards
- Reusable
- High data and image storage capacity
- Facilitator of new applications not otherwise possible

Removability is expected to be an important benefit of rewritable optical disks since it allows the transportability of data to any location. In addition, reliability will be another important selling advantage. Common with Winchester drives, the magnetic reading device, or head, of a disk drive (just 15-millionths of an inch above the disk) collides with the spinning disk and consequently loses invaluable data. There is no such chance of a head crash with a rewritable or write-once optical disk system; the laser is one-sixteenth of an inch above the optical disk which is coated with a protective layer of plastic or chemically strengthened glass.

To better appreciate the unique characteristics and features of rewritable optical disk technology, a correlation can be made with perceived benefits that result from these features as shown in Table 1 below.

Table 1. Comparison of Rewritable Optical Disk Storage Features and Benefits

Features	Benefits
Removability	Transportability Security
Cartridge	Add cartridges versus drives Reduced cost per megabyte Fewer mounts and dismounts
Erasable	Re-usable media Lower cost per megabyte
High-storage capacity	Reduced storage space and costs Lower costs for additional megabytes
Jukebox capability	Online access to data Near-line access to large databases

	Unattended operation
Large online databases	Low waiting cost High usage Unattended operations Higher productivity
Random access (compared to tape)	Faster access time Increased response time
Data security	No head crashes 10-year data life with reusability
Data interchange	Transportable media with standards Allows data interchange between sites Compatible with existing equipment

Barriers to be Resolved

Rewritable optical storage faces a number of technical hardware and software barriers before widespread market acceptance can be expected (See Table 2). Typically, the first generation of rewritable optical disk drives are competing with advanced Winchester hard disk drive systems which can hold almost as much data as a rewritable optical disk. Second-generation rewritable optical disk drives (both 5.25- and 3.5-inch) announced by Sharp, Sony and other hardware manufacturers are expected to store up to 1GB of data per erasable optical disk making them considerably more competitive with WORM, CD-ROM and magnetic data storage capacities.

Table 2. Barriers to Widespread Acceptance of Rewritable Optical Disk Storage

- Volume availability of appropriate M-O media
- Consensus on data interchange standards
- Availability of software tools, e.g., device drivers and file management software
- Multiple sources of media, hardware and software supply
- Ability of suppliers (OEMs, VARs, and system integrations) to provide adequate and timely technical support to customers
- High price of rewritable drives as compared with magnetic media

Rewritable optical media and hardware costs are an important consideration in evaluating the current and projected competitiveness of rewritable optical storage. The current cost of an erasable optical disk drive is approximately $4000 to $5000 compared with $1000 or less for the majority of Winchester hard disk drives currently on the market. In addition, the current performance of first-generation rewritable optical disk drives is still surpassed by Winchester disk drives which continue to become cheaper and faster. It is important to remember that fixed disk drives usually double their performance every two to three years.

Moreover, the cost of a single erasable optical disk is about $250 from virtually all rewritable optical disk media manufacturers such as 3M, Sony, and PDO (Philips and Du Pont Optical Company). Only NeXT, Inc. offers a $50 rewritable optical disk compatible only with a Canon drive with its workstation.

While volume availability of rewritable optical media is still somewhat limited, second and third sources of media are becoming available. As media sources become increasingly available, and drive prices continue to drop, the cost of a single rewritable optical disk can be expected to continue to drop thus lowering the cost per megabyte of storage.

Another barrier to appreciate is M-O's inherent requirement to independently erase any written sectors before any can be rewritten, introducing a latency that halves M-O's performance relative to magnetic storage. Methods for direct (single-pass) overwrite are one of the major goals of current R&D for rewritable optical recording. This capability is expected to be available within the next three years. Currently, M-O media must first be erased before it can be written over. This two-step process results in slower access time.

Another method to resolve this problem is to use effective file management software. Optotech, a subsidiary of Hewlett Packard, has suggested a possible solution to this problem and that is to decouple the erasure of a sector from the rewriting of a sector. That is, if a file system kept two lists, a "garbage list" containing sectors to be erase and a "clean list" containing sectors that are erased, writing a sector simply would consist of using sectors from the second list and thus eliminating the need for an erase pass. Deleting or modifying a sector would consist of merely placing the sector address on the garbage list. When the operating system is not busy, or at times when the user does not demand the performance, erase passes could be performed on sectors in the garbage list and returned to the clean list. This would be particularly possible in a multi-tasking environment (Beshore, 1989).

Rewritable Optical Media

Currently, there are three basic methods used for rewritable optical disk systems today: magneto-optical (M-O), dye-polymer, and phase-change. This book focuses on M-O, the rewritable optical media currently available (mid-1990) on the market today. All three of these approaches require heat which changes the physical or chemical structure of the materials in order to perform the write/erase function. Media performance is highly sensitive to impurities, oxidation, impurity diffusion and other imperfections that create defects and that often only are discernible after multiple switching cycles.

Although primarily in research and development, phase-change and dye-polymer rewritable optical media and several additional approaches to developing rewritable optical media are discussed in this section.

Magneto-Optical

Essentially, M-O is laser-assisted magnetic recording that uses the heating effect of absorbed laser light together with a magnetic field. M-O uses a plastic disk with a magnetic layer. The magnetic layer uses magnetic principles of recording for writing, reading and erasing. Digital information is stored in the form of magnetic flux directions rather than deformed physical bumps, e.g., pits and bumps.

How M-O disks works:

> Each tiny data storage spot on a blank disk is magnetized in the same direction; the magnetic field of each bit is either in a north-pole-down (digital 0) or north pole-up (digital 1) direction. The magnetic orientation cannot be changed unless the disk is heated.
>
> To write digitized information, an infrared laser rapidly heats selected data storage spots on the disk. A magnetic coil flips the north (or south) up to signify a binary "1" or leaves it point down for a binary "0". The writing magnet is strong enough so that its magnetic field cannot reverse in time for each bit that zooms by. Polarity changes once per disk rotation requiring two cycles to complete a random write even though writes on new or erased disks (which the computer knows contain all 0s) could be accomplished in one rotation. The disk drive controller automatically handles the two-step process. Setting the write-protect tab on either side of the disk cartridge ensures disk safety.
>
> The disk is able to read data as a result of the Kerr effect[1]. To read stored information, the laser bounces off the disk on a weaker setting.

> The light is polarized clockwise or counterwise depending on which way a data spot is magnetized. The disk drive deciphers the signal.
>
> To erase data the magnetic coil reverses its fields, the laser is turned on for one disk rotation, writing all 0s on the space designated for new data. During the second pass, 1s are written — where — needed to inscribe data.
>
> With the laser turned off, the heated area cools so rapidly the bit's new magnetic direction is frozen. Unless a two-ton magnet was available, at room temperature it is virtually impossible to change or erase data by accident.

M-O disks can be written to and erased repeatedly with no measurable media wear or data degradation according to a variety of accelerated laboratory-based life cycle tests performed by Sony Corporation and 3M, a leader in M-O media. Data retention of at least ten years is expected. The hard error rate is one error in 10-12 bit, and is ten times better than the error rate of 6250 one-half-inch magnetic tape.

Currently, both glass and polycarbonate substrates are used to create rewritable M-O optical disks. PDO uses glass as a substrate whereas Sony Corporation uses plastic. PDO's media comes with a twenty-five year media life warranty and can be used on Sony's M-O drives. PDO's disks are qualified for use on Sony, Ricoh, and Maxoptix rewritable drives and are fully interchangeable (read-write-erase) between these devices. Plastic substrates are more difficult to qualifier because it absorbs humidity and oxidizes, and is susceptible to warping at temperatures approach 70 degrees Centigrade. Glass is expected to be more important as rewritable optical disk drives increase to speeds of 3600 RPM.

M-O rewritable media has the durability and portability of the other optical storage media but without the drawbacks of dye-polymer and phase-change media.

Dye-Polymer

Dye-Polymer uses a translucent plastic disk with a color layer which absorbs heat from the drive's laser beam. A bump is created on the area heated by the laser. Reading such a disk is similar to reading a CD-ROM disc in which the bumps reflect light differently than the flat areas in between.

A dye-polymer rewritable optical disk drive requires two separate lasers that are different wavelengths; thus, this type of rewritable optical drive is more expensive than an M-O drive. There are additional problems with dye-polymer since the media appears to wear out after 1,000 to 10,000 write cycles.

Optical Data Inc.[2] uses dye-polymer in its flexible rewritable media. ODI licensed its media to both Tandy Corporation and Teijin, Ltd. Tandy Corporation had announced in the spring of 1988 that it would supply rewritable disks and drives using ODI's technology. The THOR-CD (Tandy High-Intensity Optical Recording CD) Project has announced its indefinite delay; Teijin, Ltd. is actively pursuing the commercialization of ODI's media.

Phase-Change

Reversible phase-change materials are the principal alternative to M-O materials for rewritable optical recording. Phase-change rewritable optical media use a plastic disk with a special metal layer. Phase-change recording and erasure are accomplished by different thermal cycles. Heat generated by the drive's laser changes the molecular structure of spots on the metal layer from an amorphous state to a crystalline state and back again. To read information off a phase-change disk, differences in the brightness of the reflected light from the amorphous spots and crystalline spots are detected. Erasure results from slower heating which anneals the media back to a polycrystalline condition.

The performance of rewritable phase-change media depends critically on composition. Problems with phase-change rewritable optical media are similar to dye-polymer media: an expensive high-powered laser is required and the media is unable to survive many rewrite cycles.

In mid-1990, Panasonic introduced a multifunction (WORM and rewritable optical disk) drive that features phase-change overwrite optical disk technology. Philips and Matsushita are among the slowly growing number of organizations developing phase-change media. In 1983, Matsushita demonstrated a 3.5-inch phase-change rewritable media and licensed certain patents from Energy Conversion Devices (Troy, MI) devised by Stanford R. Ovshinsky. Other licensees include Hitachi, IBM, Sony, and Asahi Chemical Company. ECD's phase-change method is already in use in several WORM products. Specifically, this phase-change disk drive includes the ability to overwrite directly with a single laser beam compared with other phase-change materials which require a two-laser beam: one in a round shape to record, and a second in an oval shape for simultaneous erasing.

Alternative Rewritable Optical Media

As stated above, a problem facing both magneto-optical and phase-change materials is the affect that repeated thermal cycling has on their durability. Optex Corporation, formed in 1986 to develop an erasable optical memory system, is developing a rewritable optical disk and drive using Quantex Corporation's Electron Trapping Optical Memory (ETOM™) technology. Based on photonics, ETOM is a new computer storage medium which uses phosphor materials and operates using the phenomenon of electron trapping. Electrons are trapped when the material is illuminated with short-wavelength light. Subsequent illumination with infrared light causes the trapped electronics to be released. Data patterns written on the medium with blue (short-wavelength) light can then be read with infrared light. Optex has completed a 100 million read, write and erase cycle test of its ETOM disk and reported the absence of any material degradation or change in the physical characteristics of the media.

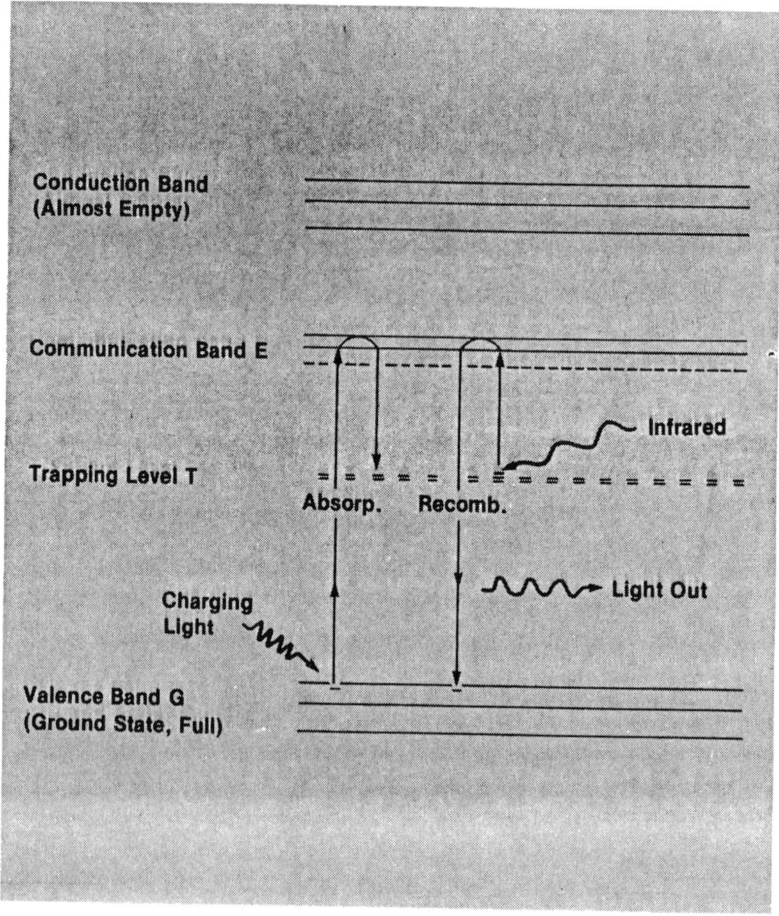

Figure 1. Schematic of electron trapping phenomenon. (Courtesy, Optex Corporation).

Designed by Vision Three, Inc., the ETOM drive has a potential read/write speed of 4 megabits per second. According to the Optex, the ETOM drive is faster than the 2.8 megabit maximum transfer rate typically found with first-generation M-O drives. The first commercially available product is expected to be introduced by the end of 1991.

N.V. Philips (Eindhoven, Netherlands) is experimenting with several rare earth metals in order to develop a rewritable optical media. IBM is developing a method called spectral-hole burning which offers exceptionally high data density (100 to 1000 times greater than conventional optical recording) but faces a variety of problems including cryogenic operating conditions, limited number of readout cycles, and the need for a special laser (Marchant, 1989).

Rewritable Optical Drives

All commercially available rewritable optical disk products currently employ M-O technology. The first M-O disk drive for the North American market was introduced in the spring of 1988 by Sony Corporation. Canon, Ricoh, Hitachi, Literal Corporation (formerly LaserDrive Ltd.), and Maxoptix (a joint venture of Maxtor and Kubota) have introduced similar products. Table 3 offers a comparison of first-generation rewritable M-O optical disk drives. The average access times and data transfer rates reported are subject to variations associated with particular implications of a given product.

Today's rewritable optical disk drives have relatively low access speeds compared with current magnetic storage. Although faster than most WORM optical drives, rewritable optical disk drives are considerably slower than fixed magnetic hard disks which have an average access time under 30 milliseconds. By the end of 1990, Sony and Ricoh will offer second-generation (5.25- and 3.5-inch) rewritable optical disk drives with faster access times and transfer rates as well as considerably greater storage capacity. Cache buffering and a dual part buffer are expected to be available with Ricoh's new rewritable optical drive.

Data storage capacity is now between 600MBs per disk up to 1GB depending upon whose drive is being used. Storage capacities vary depending upon formatting methods. Sony, Ricoh, and Hitachi rewritable drives can store 297MBs per side or 594MBs per double-sided disks formatted with 512KBs per sector. If the same cartridges are formatted with 1024KBs per sector, their storage capacity increases to 325MBs per recording surface or 650MBs per double-sided cartridge. The Maxoptix Tahiti 1 drive, compatible with ISO standard media in 594MB and 650MB storage formats, also supports a Zoned-Constant Angular Velocity (ZCAV) which is actually the MCAV (Modified Constant Angular Velocity) recording method. Considered a high-performance drive, Tahiti 1 offers 466MBs per side for disks formatted with 512KBs per sector and 512MBs per side with disks formatted with 1024KBs per sector. The ZCAV recording method requires Maxtor's 1GB rewritable optical disks. Canon, on the other hand, offers less than half the recording capacity of competing products.

Table 3. Comparison of First-Generation Rewritable Optical Disk Drives

Vendor	Interface	Controller Memory	Data Transfer Rates Burst/Sustained	Capacity Per Side	Seek Times max/avg/track
Sony SMO D-501	SCSI modified EDSI	64KB	1.2MB/680MB	297/325MB	180/90/20
Canon OM 500D	SCSI modified EDSI	64KB	1.5MB/260MB	256MB	92/130/10
Hitachi OD-112-1	SCSI	64KB	1.5MB/—	297/325MB	—/62.5/—
Matsushita JU-9500	SCSI, EDSI	—	—/925KB	300MB	—/75/—
Maxtor Tahiti 1	SCSI	—	4MB/1.25MB	466/512MB 298/326MB	70/35/1
Ricoh RO-5030E	SCSI	256KB	1.2MB/300MB	297/326MB	—/44/—
Sharp JY-500	SCSI	—	2.4MB/150KB	325MB	200/67/—

All M-O erasable drives use the 5.25-inch disk encapsulated in protective plastic "caddy" similar to WORM optical disks. All rewritable optical disk drives (except for the Canon system) can accommodate double-sided ISO-standard M-O cartridges.

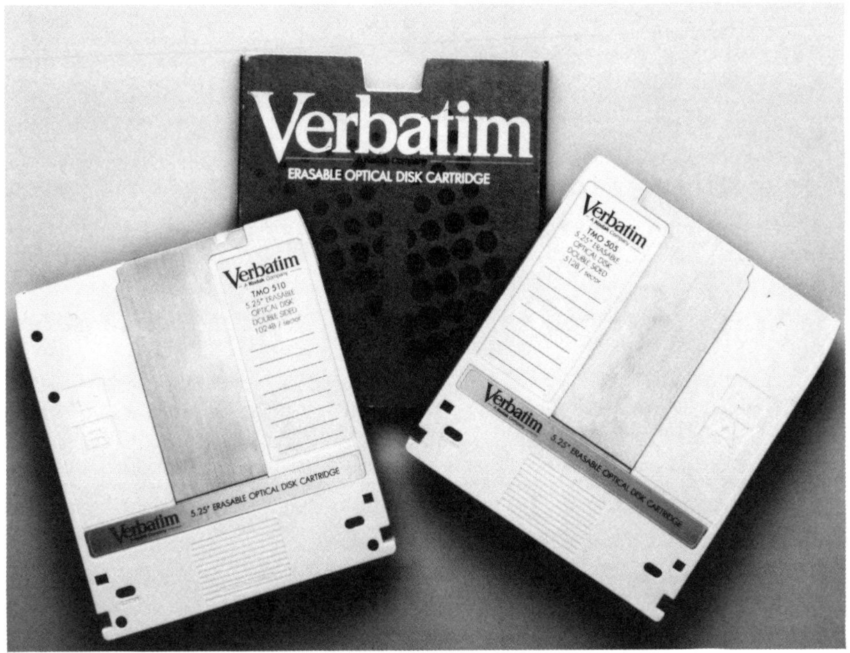

The TMO 5.25-inch disk initially announced was to be available in two versions: the Model 510 (left) contains 1025KBs per sector, and the Model 505 (right) contains 512KBs per sector. Both versions were to be double-sided with a user capacity of more than 300,000 pages of text. (Courtesy, Literal Corporation)

Since the introduction of the first M-O drive in 1988, primarily Sony, Maxtor and Ricoh drives have been integrated in a growing number of "plug-and-play" subsystems available from VARs, system integrators and other OEMs. Products are now available for MS-DOS, OS/2, NeXT, SCO Xenix, Unibus- and Q-bus computers, VAX/VMS, Unix, Sun, and Macintosh environments.

Fujitsu has developed an 8-inch M-O rewritable optical disk system that uses a fixed drive. Prototypes have a data access time of 3.3 seconds compared with jukebox access times today (the Cygnet 5.25-inch Model 5250 has an access time is approximately 4 seconds). Future enhancements to this device will provide an increased data transfer rate, high-power laser diode, parallel transfer to and from the two optical heads, direct overwrite, and elimination of read after write. In addition, data access time will be increased and optical heads will be smaller and lightweight.

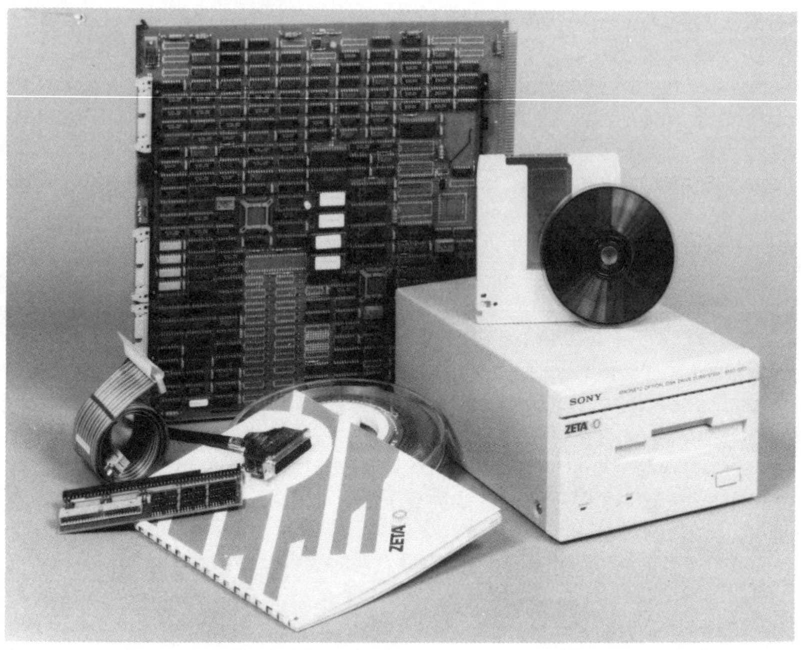

The Model SKR-600 is a rewritable optical subsystem compatible with Data General's MV series of minicomputers. It includes a Sony M-O 5.25-inch rewritable disk drive, a Data General-emulating disk controller, and a SCSI cable. (Courtesy, Zetaco Corporation)

Several manufacturers such as Sony and Literal Corporation (owned by Eastman Kodak Company, Olivetti & CO., S.P..A., and Kawasaki Steel Corporation) have also demonstrated 3.5-inch M-O drives but these are not yet commercially available. Literal Corporation's 3.5-inch M-O media holds 60MBs (formatted) of data and has a 30 milliseconds average seek time. The TMO 35/60 comes as a complete media-hardware package in which the subsystem with drive, power supply, and SCSI controller card are in a box that fits under most monitors. Software drivers are available for IBM-PC/AT/XT computers and for the Apple Macintosh Plus, SE and II models. Each TMO 3.5-inch disk has over 10,000 concentric tracks of which 9727 are for user data; the disk surface is divided into thirteen sectors with 512KBs each. These 3.5-inch M-O disk drives are expected to be widely popular with low-end/low-performance PC-based systems by the mid-1990s.

Multifunction Optical Disk Drives

A variety of Japanese manufacturers have announced their intention to manufacture multifunction or hybrid drives, and a number of them have already introduced products both in Japan and the U.S.: Pioneer, Sony, NTT (Nippon Telephone and Telegraph), and Kokusai Denshin Denwa Company Ltd. (KDD). In 1988, NTT demonstrated an early prototype of a multifunction drive at an IEEE conference.

While phase-change and write-once optical media are considered more compatible than M-O and write-once media for use in a multifunction drive, there are as of yet few announced products or plans for developing drives which include phase-change media. Literal Corporation plans to manufacture 5.25-inch multifunction optical drives using phase-change media. At the spring 1990 COMDEX show, Panasonic Communications and Systems Company announced a 5.25-inch multifunction optical disk drive which uses direct overwrite phase-change technology. According to specifications released in June 1990, the LF-7010 has a storage capacity of 500MB per side, and can both read and write to Panasonic's currently available WORM media. The LF-7010 does not conform to ISO/ANSI proposed standards for magneto-optic technology; also, it is important to note that there are currently no standards for a phase-change overwrite optical disk drive.

Pioneer has developed a multifunction drive, the DE-U7001, which offers write-once and rewritable functions. Pioneer's drive was first introduced in Japan and is now available in the U.S. This drive will be sold by LMSI and Optimem as well as Pioneer. It conforms to an ISO draft for sampled servo format; it has a 327MBs storage capacity per disk side and uses Pioneer's currently available WORM media. In addition, Sony Corporation plans to offer a multifunction optical disk drive which combines a read-only optical disk drive with a rewritable M-O device. Other firms which have announced multifunction drives include Ricoh which is demonstrating a 5.25-inch "dual function" (write-once and rewritable) drive, the RO-5042, in Japan. It is expected that Maxtor will eventually market the Ricoh multifunction optical disk drive in the U.S. as part of a subsystem sometime in 1991.

Rewritable M-O videodisc systems will be introduced in the next year by several major optical storage companies. Pioneer and KDD have announced a jointly developed rewritable M-O videodisc system that is capable of storing up to thirty minutes of motion video or 54,000 still frames in the analog LaserDisc™ format. According to Pioneer this system offers 400 lines of horizontal resolution, two-channel FM sound, video S/N of more than 45dB, average access speed of 0.2 seconds using a high-speed access mechanism that separates reading optics, and a pre-formatted address control and an RS-232C interface and protocols that are compatible with commercial Pioneer analog videodisc players. Initial markets will be broadcasting and other commercial producers as well as those involved in the development process of standard videodiscs.

A similar rewritable M-O videodisc system has been announced by Sony Corporation who expects to commercialize for industrial applications in the next twenty-four months for under $30,000.

Standards for Rewritable Optical Storage

ANSI (American National Standards Institute) is working on two proposed national standards: CCS (Continuous Composite Servo) and SS (Sampled Servo) for 5.25-inch (130 mm) rewritable optical disks. ANSI has also begun work on developing a standard for rewritable 3.5-inch disks as well. Each of these formats accommodates both WORM and rewritable optical disks. Generally, all rewritable optical disk drives, except for the Canon M-O non-ISO standard drive, use the CCS format.

The ANSI 5.25-inch rewritable optical disk standards project is based on the 5.25-inch WORM CCS but there are a few differences to account for the M-O nature of the read-write process. The goal of the X3B11 committee

- **Physical Cartridge Dimensions**

  Cartridge format defined = ISO draft standard

  Same as 5.25" WORM cartridge

- **Physical Media Format**

  Agreement reached on all technical issues for Continuous Composite format in ANSI (X3B11) and ISO committees (January '89)

  Manufacturers supporting Continuous Composite:

  Hewlett-Packard, Hitachi, Maxtor, Olympus/Ricoh, Philips/DuPont Optical, Sony, 3M

  Manufacturers supporting Sampled Servo:

  LMSI, Pioneer

  Manufacturers supporting proprietary formats:

  Canon, Maxtor

Figure 2. 5.25-inch Rewritable Optical Standards. (Courtesy, Hewlett Packard, Greeley Storage Division)

is to allow a multifunction optical disk drive that could handle both WORM and rewritable CCS media.

The optical rewritable standard documents include a fairly extensive chapter on defect management which details how a scheme for defective sector retirement should be implemented (Hallam, 1989).

Three of the four manufacturers currently shipping rewritable optical drives — Sony, Ricoh and Maxoptix — and optical media manufacturers — 3M and PDO (Philips and Du Pont Optical) — are committed to ANSI/ISO compatibility. According to International Development Corporation (IDC), ISO-compliant rewritable disk drives make up 95 percent of the market. Canon is the outstanding M-O drive manufacturer who does not accept the international standard.

Interchangeability is one of *the* key standards issues to resolve. Although standards will allow data interchange between different manufacturers' products, data interchange is still all but impossible between currently available units (Apiki and Eglowstein, 1989). For example, although the Ricoh rewritable optical disk drive can read Sony M-O disks, the Sony drive cannot read Ricoh M-O disks.

DATA INTERCHANGE
Standards

Size	Write-once (Slow - no consensus)	Rewritable (Fast - small size)
14 Inch	In process - slow (Few suppliers)	No activity
12 Inch	In process - slow (No consensus)	No activity
5 1/4 Inch	In process - 2 formats • ANSI - 1990 • ISO - 1990	Almost completed • ANSI - 1990 • ISO - 1990
3 1/2 Inch	No activity	In process • ANSI - 1992 • ISO - 1992

Table 4. Data Interchange Standards. (Courtesy, Sony Corporation of America)

Media interchangeability between ANSI/ISO compliant drives will allow customers to use any ANSI/ISO media rather than rely on a single proprietary media source. PDO, Sony, and 3M manufacture rewritable media that comply with ANSI/ISO standards which allow for media interchangeability.

Optical and Magnetic Competition With Rewritable Optical Disk

CD Versus Rewritable

The general consensus is that the most effective use of CD-ROM technology is as a low-cost distribution and publishing read-only optical device. CD disks store graphical information, data, audio/music, full-motion video, and still images. CD-ROM has a high-storage capacity (up to 600-650MBs per disc), permanence, fast production, and a low production cost per unit. Since its requirement for high-cost mastering and replication equipment, CD-ROM is not feasible for limited distribution requirements. It is impossible to write on a read-only CD-ROM since it requires three production major steps: data conversion, premastering, and mastering/replication. Current applications of CD-ROM include reference, substitution for online databases, education and training, publishing, financial data, software manuals, parts catalog, software distribution, maps, and an alternative to online access.

Compared with CD-ROM, rewritable has a lower data storage capacity (as of late 1989), is not permanent, and has a high media cost of $250. A single CD-ROM replicated disc can cost $2.00 or less. There is no need for an outside data conversion and mastering process for creating a rewritable optical disk. While it has been described by many as a potential distribution medium, it is unlikely that rewritable optical disks would serve as primary storage given there is a likelihood of loss or "accidental" erasure.

Sony and Philips have jointly developed (and announced) CD-WO (CD/Write-Once) and CD-EROM which is a CD format erasable dye-based optical media. Sony, 3M, Hitachi and other media vendors are actively developing CD/M-O media. Sony Corporation of America and the North American unit of Philips N.V. are jointly developing the specifications for a rewritable CD-ROM optical disk drive code-named "Orange Book." Although CD-ROM is read-only memory, the forthcoming new generation CD drive would be capable of overwriting new media that could also be read by conventional CD-ROM drives. An audio version of the rewritable CD is expected to be completed and released in 1991; the data version of this drive could be available as early as 1992.

However, it is important to understand that rewritable CDs face four significant and major technical barriers:

- Creating a media surface for environmental stability
- Developing media to support EFM code
- Provide media absolute reflectivity compatibility (pit jitter)
- Radial tracking problems

Rewritable CDs are expected to have backward compatibility with CD audio applications. Based upon today's prototype drives and ongoing work to further increase storage capacities, CD-WO disks will eventually have a 1GB storage capacity to effectively competing with today's 5.25-inch WORM and rewritable optical disks.

Write-Once Versus Rewritable

The single common factor between WORM and rewritable optical media and drives is that both use lasers to store densely packed information on a removable optical disk. The two technologies use different media, different recording and reading schemes, and have different applications and uses. WORM is available in a variety of formats: 5.25-, 12-, and 14-inch whereas rewritable is currently available in 5.25-inch format and will eventually be available in 3.5-inch and smaller.

Write-once means that data can be written to a disk only once and cannot be erased; it is permanently stored. WORM has a perception of being a more secure media. It suits the archive objective of being non-rewritable and has an expected shelf life of at least ten to thirty years.

WORM applications include backup, archival storage and retrieval, engineering drawings and documentation, medical image storage and retrieval, automating office functions such as personnel records management, reporting, and correspondence. WORM systems are currently being used in law, engineering, banks, insurance, transportation, and university admissions. WORM disks have a larger storage capacity and a relatively fast random access retrieval capacity compared with first-generation rewritable optical disk systems. By nature, they are useful for incremental backups or for storing databases that must be regularly updated. Another area of difference is media cost. Rewritable disks cost almost twice as much as WORM optical disks.

Rewritable will be competitive with WORM depending on how long data must be stored unchanged. According to InfoCorp, if data being man-

MASS STORAGE APPLICATIONS

VARIABLES (5 1/4")	WINCHESTER	WORM	REWRITABLE
Capacity/MB	661	600	644
Access time - w/ latency - w/o latency	 24.3 16.0	 110 93	 75.0 62.5
$ Cost drive	2000	3787	3940
$ Cost/MB	3.02	6.31	6.11
$ additional/4627 MB	3.02	.33	.61
*$ additional/28.8 GB	3.02	.916	1.38
Data transfer rate KB/sec	2458	690	925
SCSI Transfer Rate	1.5	1.5	1.5
MTBF (hrs.)	40,000	20,000	20,000

(*based on 5 1/4" - 48 cartridge library cost-OEM)

Table 5. Comparison of Mass Storage Characteristics. (Courtesy, Hitachi Computer Division)

aged has a shelf life of six months or less, then the application could convert to rewritable drives and media. If the information must be kept more than three years, users are unlikely to be concerned about recycling media.

If information must be stored between six months and three years, the preference for recyclable media will depend on the economic trade-offs of having information on unchangeable media versus the economics of rewritable including the costs of managing the recycling operation. It is expected that WORM will be more vulnerable to replacement rewritable optical disk drives in financial applications that require data storage between six months and three years.

Table 6. Comparison of Magnetic, Write-Once and Rewritable Optical Disk Applications

Winchester†	**WORM**	**Rewritable**
Rewritable	————	Rewritable
————	Removable	Removable
————	Transportable	Transportable
Low $MB/drive	Med $MB/drive	High $MB/drive
————	Data Interchange	Data Interchange
Database Size	Database Size	Database Size
————	Data Security	Data Security
————	Archival Life	Archival Life
————	Legal Documents	————
Library Storage	Library Storage	Library Storage
High $MB/Library	Low $MB/Library	Low $MB/Library

†Fixed Disk only.
Courtesy, Hitachi Computer Division

Magnetic Storage Versus Rewritable

The price performance of rewritable optical disk is becoming competitive with erasable magnetic storage although it must overcome a slower transfer rate and data access time, and, for now, a lower cost per megabyte. Currently, magnetic is the primary data storage peripheral for most applications. Rewritable optical storage will eventually have a significant impact on data-intensive applications as media prices decline, and thus be more cost-effective. In additional, rewritable optical disk is removable and subsequently allows jukebox integration. Rewritable optical disk offers data security and transportability not available with most magnetic-based systems. And, perhaps most importantly for small system users, there is no possibility of head crashes. Removable hard disks such as the Bernoulli Box have a relatively low storage capacity and are not sufficiently durable for mailing and frequent handling.

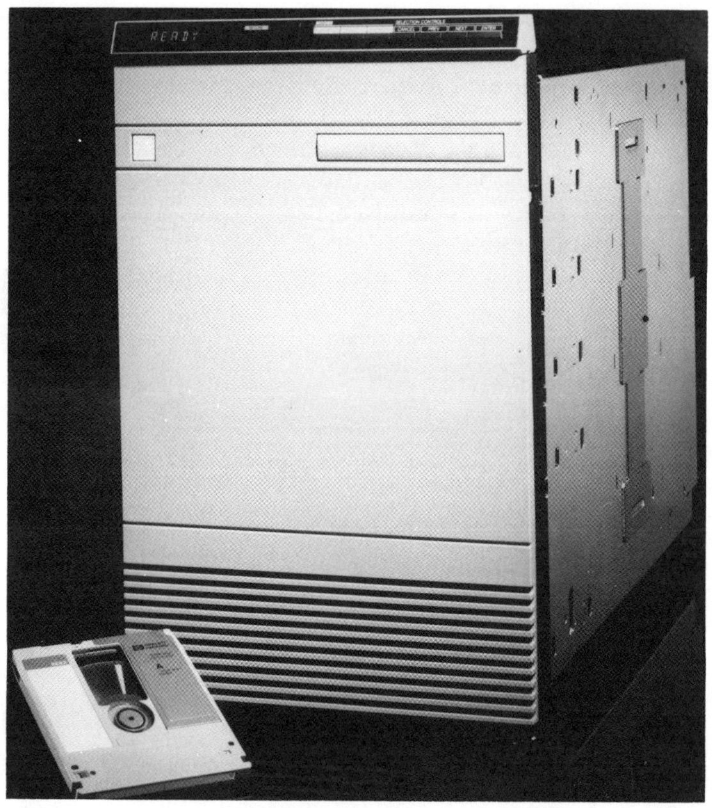

Hewlett-Packard's Rewritable Optical Disk Autochanger. (Courtesy, Hewlett-Packard, Greeley Storage Division)

Markets for Rewritable Optical Storage

Rewritable optical disk systems are starting to compete with magnetic tape subsystems for data backup and with Bernoulli box systems, removable Winchester cartridge drives. To a lesser extent, rewritable optical disk is beginning to compete with WORM optical disk drives in certain data archiving applications.

A list of target applications for rewritable optical disk includes

- PC and workstation add-on
- Images: medical, engineering, prepress/publishing
- Graphics: CAD/CAM/CAE and publishing
- Document management: insurance, medical, personnel records, and financial
- System back-up/secondary storage device
- Data distribution
- Data archival
- LAN file server
- Large archival databases
- Data security
- Desktop publishing

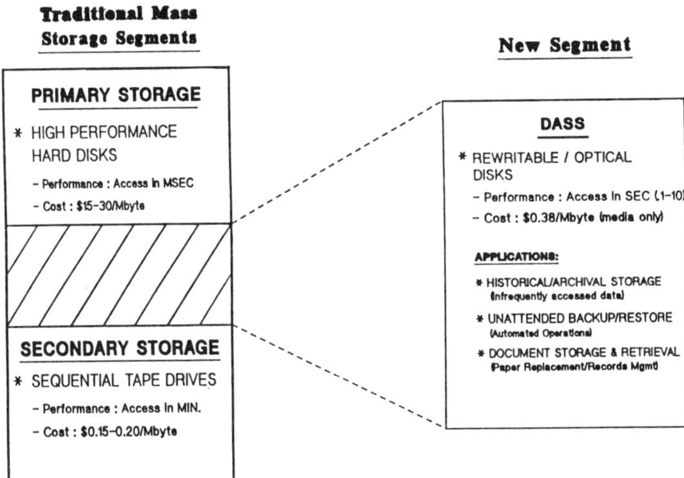

Figure 3. Direct Access Secondary Storage. (Courtesy, Hewlett-Packard, Greeley Storage Division)

Vendors of rewritable optical disk manufacturers categorize the potential market as follows:

Small Systems: entry level workstation, desktop and PC publishing, system disk, primary and secondary storage, and data interchange/distribution.

Medium-Sized Systems: Supermicrocomputers, primary and secondary storage, fault-tolerant backup, near-line storage, and data interchange/distribution.

Large Systems: Secondary storage, near-line storage, and data interchange/distribution.

There is no doubt that rewritable optical storage is an important secondary computer storage device. It is ideal for data backup because of its sustained data throughput speed and the minimal amount of operator intervention required as compared with magnetic tape.

Summary

Eventually, it will be cost and performance competitive with CD-WO and today's 5.25-inch WORM disks as well as fixed magnetic disk drives.-once and read-only) and magnetic storage. During the next few years, magnetic storage will continue to display high-performance and low-cost. Rewritable optical disk technology may well play technological and price leapfrog with magnetic storage throughout this decade.

It is important to consider the lessons learned by NeXT, Inc. which introduced its first workstation with the Canon rewritable optical drive as the primary storage device. After considerable complaints concerning the drive's slow access times and its drag on workstation performance, NeXT sent a 40MB Quadram hard disk drive to all of its end-users.

For now, it seems that the most appropriate utilization of rewritable optical disk technology will be for downloading software, archival databases and backup, and software distribution. Tape will not be replaced by rewritable optical disk but can be expected to compete in certain image-intensive and workstation-based environments such as CAD/CAE. Rewritable optical disks may well become in certain instances the secondary storage backup source for workstations using high-performance Winchester hard disk or tape drives.

The learning curve for rewritable optical disk technology is remarkedly high given its recent introduction. There are over 50 subsystems now available for a wide variety of computers. Typical roadblocks to a new storage device's market acceptance are software development efforts, recording standards, availability of drives and media, and the production of host adapters and software drivers. While software is still a challenge, the industry is now starting to write sfotware that treats WORM drives as non-erasable ones rather than earlier generation programs that attempt to trick the host into believing it was working with a magnetic drive. In addition, standards are emerging for CCS M-O disks and drives.

The growing maturity of write-once optical storage and CD technologies are bound to help foster the perception that optical storage including rewritable optical disk is a solid and realistic alternative to traditional computer storage devices.

The Inspire series is one of the first line of rewritable optical storage systems introduced. Designed to support DEC and Sun workstations as well as PC- and AT-bus, the Inspire line offers a variety of software products engineered to enhance the performance of the rewritable optical disk drive. (Courtesy, Alphatronix, Inc.)

As write-once, rewritable and read-only optical technologies are merged into multifunction or hybrid optical disk drives, their competition with one another will be diminished over the long-term. Backward compatibility, software tools, alternative and established media sources, data interchangeability standards, and transportability will continue to be critical challenges to the optical storage industry, especially rewritable optical storage if it is to change the computer industry's current storage and retrieval practices.

Directory of Organizations and Individuals Working with Rewritable Optical Storage

3M Company
Optical Recording Department
Building 225-4S-09
St. Paul, MN 55144
800/328-1300
Write-once and rewritable optical disk media manufacturer.
Offers rewritable disk capable of storing up to 650MB per disk side.

Accell Computer Corporation
17145 Bon
Karman Avenue, Suite 110
Irvine, CA 92714
714/757-1212
Offer rewritable optical storage subsystem for Macintosh users. Especially suited for computer-aided design, engineering and manufacturing (CAD/CAM/CAE) multiple-image applications and can be used as a storage device in a LAN operating server system.

ACS Systemberatung GmbH
Poststrasse 33
2 Hamburg 36
West Germany
+49-40-350-8000
Data processing and communications firm offers HYPARCHIV document image software. It supports a wide range of optical storage devices including Ricoh and Sony M-O 5.25-inch drives.

Absoft Corporation
2781 Bond Street

Rochester Hills, MI 48309
313/853-0050
FORTRAN 77 compiler is optimized to run on the NeXT workstation and allows porting programs written for the VAX/VMS, IBM/VS, Sun and Apollo machines to the NeXT. Supports version 0.9 of the NeXT operating system.

Advanced Decision System
1500 Plymouth Street
Mountain View, CA 94043
415/960-7300
Developing networking application of Jasmine's DirectOptical rewritable drive.

Advanced Graphic Applications, Inc. (AGA)
90 Fifth Avenue
New York, NY 10011-7696
212/337-4200
DISCUS (Data, Image, Sound, Communications Unified Storage) is available as a write-once and rewritable optical storage system for the IBM-PC and PS/2 and compatibles under OS/2 and DOS.

Offers DISCUS Rewritable jukebox for MS-DOS, OS/2 and SCO Xenix installations; it can store up to 56 M-O disk cartridges and offers approximately 35GBs of online storage capacity.

Alphatronix, Inc.
4900 Prospectus Drive, Suite 1000
POB 13687
Research Triangle Park, NC 27709
919/544-0001
Developed Inspire, an rewritable subsystem, for DEC, Sun and IBM-compatible computers based on the Sony rewritable drive. Offers a jukebox configuration for the Inspire subsystem for DEC and Sun workstations as well as AT-based PCs. Bypass is a software product that allows the user to use the same disk in a VAX and PC environment.

Rapidstore backs up files up to five times faster than 6250 BPI tape, operates as a normal VMS disk, initializes disk on-the-fly, defragments files and supports wildcard operations for file and directory selection.

Ambertek Systems, Inc.
POB 7124
Thousand Oaks, CA 91359
805/493-1595
Marketing optical subsystems based on Sony's 12-inch WORM and rewrita-

ble optical drives for the IBM-PC and compatible systems; DEC VAX versions are under development.

American Digital Systems
490 Boston Post Road
Sudbury, MA 01776
508/443-7711
Offers the Masterdisk Optical, a rewritable optical storage sub system which operates with all DEC Qbus, Unibus, 3100 series- and Bi-Bus-based systems.

American Image and Information Management (AIIM)
1101 Wayne Avenue, Suite 1100
Silver Spring, MD 20016
202/537-7716
Trade association.

American National Standards Institute (ANSI)
Accredit Standards Committee X3
c/o Howard Kaikow
Digital Equipment Corporation
110 Spit Brook Road
Mail Stop KZ03-4/Z090
Nashua, New Hampshire
603/881-1122
X3B11.1 is responsible for developing optical disk volume and file structure standards which will facilitate the interface of information on removable optical disks.

American National Standards Institute, Inc. (ANSI)
1430 Broadway
New York, NY 10018
212/642-4900
Organization associated with standards for all industries. Publishes the official SCSI standard specification. X3B11 is the standards committee involved with establishing optical media and drive standards. See ENDL Associates.

Apex Systems, Inc.
5785 Arapahoe Road, Suite D
Boulder, CO 80303
303/443-3393
Offers optical head/media testers for WORM and M-O rewritable media, as well as optical head characterization.

Applied Magnetics Corporation
Optical Products Division
18960 Base Camp Road
Monument, CO 80132
303/488-2900
Signed an agreement with Hewlett-Packard to use certain Hp patents and expertise relating to M-O recording heads. Firm is currently developing a line of optical recording heads and subassemblies.

Apunix Computer Services
9330 Carmel Mountain Road, Suite C
San Diego, CA 92129
619/484-0074
Offers the APD-650M-CN-S subsystem using Ricoh's 5.25-inch M-O drive.

Aquidneck Systems International
650 Ten Rod Road
North Kingstown, RI 02852
401/295-2691
The Sony 5.25-inch M-O rewritable drive to the list of qualified optical drives supported under its OAS 100 and 3400 Series data storage subsystems.

Arix Computer Coprporation
821 Fox Lane
San Jose, CA 95131
408/432-1200
The RO-5030E subsystem uses a Ricoh 5.25-inch rewritable optical disk drive with a SCSI interface.

Artecon, Inc.
2440 Impala Drive
Box 9000, Department 5500
Carlsbad, CA 92008-0993
619/931-5500
Systems integrator. Offers rewritable optical disk drive subsystem for Sun 3 Microsystems workstations using Sony M-O drive; subsystem runs on Sun OS 4.0.1 operating system with either Sun 3 or Sun 2 SCSI host adapter.

Asaca/Shibasoku
Uses M-O disk to store up to 1600 frames of color still-store image data per 5.25-inch double-sided disk. The ADS-300 mainframe is also capable of controlling up to seven external dual-disk drives for a maximum online data bank

of 11,200 frames.

Battelle Pacific Northwest Laboratories
Battelle Blvd.
Richland, WA 99352
509/375-3688
Developed rewritable optical recording and storage medium for which the patent was assigned to Optical Data, Inc.

Berg Software Design
P.O. Box 3488
Saratoga, CA 95070
408/741-5710
Consulting firm specializing in UNIX and DOS device drivers and applications software for CD-ROM, WORM and rewritable optical storage.

Brenco Computer Systems, Inc.
520 Fellowship Road, Suite 208
Mt. Laurel, NJ 08054
609/722-5600
Offers subsystem for IBM-PC/AT, PS/2 and compatible computers. Villanova University (Philadelphia, PA) was one of the first end-users of a Brenco subsystem.

BusinessLand, Inc.
1001 Ridder Park Drive
San Jose, CA 95131
408/437-0400
The only retail computer store chain to offer the NeXT Computer.

Canon America, Inc.
One Canon Plaza
Lake Success, NY 10042-1113
516/488-6700
5.25-inch rewritable drive and media manufacturer. Investor in NeXT, Inc. and marketing NeXT computer in the Far East.Offering a desktop electronic filing system based on M-O technology. The Canofile 250 offers a storage capacity of 256MB per disk side and incorporates a LCD, digital rotary scanner, keyboard and laser printer.

Marketing its M-O disk drive as a complete subsystem for IBM-compatible and Macintosh. With 250MB of single-sided recording capacity, the MO-5001S offers less than half the storage capacity of double-sided M-O disk systems manufactured by Sony, Ricoh, Maxtor and other firms.

Canon, Ltd.,
Information Systems
The Fleming Centre, United 1A
Fleming Way, Crawley
West Sussex RH10 2MM United Kingdom
0293-561180
WORM and rewritable drive manufacturer; supplier of rewritable drive in the NeXT computer.

CAP International
One Longworth Circle
Norwell, MA 02061
617/982-9500
Market research and consulting.

Carlisle Memory Products
10170 Sorrento Valley Road
San Diego, CA 92121
619/452-7840
Markets 5.25-inch WORM and rewritable disks as well as 3.5-inch rewritable disks manufactured by Daicel Chemical.

CBEMA (Computer and Business Equipment Manufacturers Association)
311 First Street, N.W.
Suite 500
Washington, D.C. 20001-2178
202.737.8888
IIndustry trade group administers the Approved Standards Committees (ASCs) which work on projects intended to become standards of ANSI.

Centel Federal Systems
11400 Commerce Park Drive
Reston, VA 22091
703.758.7000
Offers systems integration, connectivity, tempesting, security, network services for WORM, rewritable and CD-ROM optical storage.

CIMTECH (National Centre for Information Media and Technology)
POB 109, College Lane
Hatfield, Herts
AL10 9AB United Kingdom
0707-279670
Publishers of the journal *Information Media and Technology*, sponsors conferences and seminars, and offers consulting in micrographics, videotex, CD-ROM, WORM and rewritable optical storage as well as desktop publishing and word processing.

Cohasset Associates
505 North Lake Shore Drive
Chicago, IL 60611
312/527-1550
Publishers of *The Legality of Optical Storage* and sponsor of Optical Storage Laws and Regulations conference.

Computer Peripherals Division
991 Knox Street
Torrance, CA 90502
213/515-3993
5.25-inch WORM and rewritable drive, and jukebox manufacturer.

Concurrent Computer Corporation
106 Apple Street
Tinton Falls, NJ 07724
800/631/2154
The R/W optical subsystem uses a maxtor 5.25-inch rewritable disk drive.

Consan, Inc.
14625 Martin Drive
Eden Prairie, MN 55344
612/949-0053
The RS600/N subsystem intergrates a Ricoh 5.25-inch rewritable disk drive.

Corning Glass Works
Precision Molded Optics
Sullivan Park, WW-01-8
Corning, New York 14831
607/974-3495
Manufacturer of glass disk media substrates for rewritable and write-once optical storage.

Cygnet Systems, Inc.
2560 Junction Avenue
San Jose, CA 95013
408/954-1800
Latest offering is a 5.25-inch rewritable optical jukebox, and the industry's first one-year comprehensive warranty for its full line of optical disk jukeboxes. Offers a line of 12-inch and 5.25-inch WORM optical jukeboxes. Jukebox Interface Management System (JIMS) is a software package.

Cygnet Systems, Inc.
10480 Little Patuxent Parkway
Suite 400
Columbia, MD 21044
301/740-8754

Daicel (USA), Inc.
611 West Sixth Street
Suite 2152
Los Angeles, CA 90017
213/629-3656
Write-once and rewritable optical disk media manufacturer: 12-, 8-, 5.25-, and 3.5-inch.

Dartmouth College
Language Resource Center
201 Bartlett Hall
Hanover, New Hampshire 03755
603/646-2624
Using Jasmine rewritable optical disk drive for backup and CD-ROM test production.

Data Systems Technology
585 Burbank, Suite A
Broomfield, CO 80020
303/466-5228
Offers custom optical controller development for 5.25-inch and 3.5-inch rewritable and WORM storage drives.

Decade Computers, Ltd.
Unity House
Kennetside, Newbury

Berks RG14 5PX United Kingdom
0635-38008
European distributor of the Alphatronix INSPIRE rewritable optical disk mass to rage system.

DEI
10170 Sorrento Valley Road
San Diego, CA 92121-1604
619/452-7840
Distributor of Daicel Chemical magneto-optic rewritable and WORM media in the U.S.

Deltraic Systems
1977 O'Toole Avenue, Suite B206
San Jose, CA 95131
408/954-1055
Offers two systems: OptiServer 600 subsystem with a Ricoh 5.25-inch rewritable optical disk drive.

Distributed Logic Corporation (Dilog)
1555 South Sinclair Street
Anaheim, CA 92806
714/937-5700
Offers a rewritable optical storage subsystem for DEC !-Bus and Univus users and SCSI interface.

Dimensional Visions Group
718 Arch Street
Suite 202 North
Philadelphia, PA 19106
215/337-4686
Storing graphic images on Jasmine rewritable drive.

Disk Equipment and Materials Association (DEMA)
c/o Material Progress Corporation
POB 5824
Santa Rosa, CA 95402-5824
707/527-6100

Disk/Trend Report
1925 Landings Drive
Mountain View, CA 94043

415/961-6209
Consulting, market research and analyses, and co-sponsor of annual Data-Storage conference.

Dolphin Systems Technology
1701 East Edinger Avenue
Building G
Santa Ana, CA 92705
714/558-3220
Sonar 600 rewritable optical subsystem for Macintosh, Sun and IBM-PC microcomputers. Stand-alone unit uses Sony M-O drive.

E. I. DuPont Nemours, Inc.
Imaging Systems Department
Eagle Run
POB 6099
Newark, DE 19702
302/733-9455
FastTrax is an engineering drawing and related-documents management system that integrates a scanner, rewritable and WORM drive, and hard disk. It is a computerized graphic database that creates a bit-mapped (raster) representation of engineering, architectural and other types of drawings. It stores associated documents and textual information related to drawings. Opti-Safe is an optical archival system for the printing and graphic arts industry.

Dynatek Automation Systems, Inc.
15 Tangiers Road
Toronto, Ontario
M3j 2B1 Canada
416/646-3000
Offers three subsystems using Ricoh's 5.25-inch M-O drive.

Electronic Data Systems Corporation
7171 Forest Lane
Dallas, TX 75230
214/661-6188
Systems integrator in banking/financial, federal government, insurance, health care, manufacturing, retail, state and local governments, transportation, utilities, international communications, and wholesale/distribution markets.

Electronic Data Systems Corporation
Demand Services Division

13600 EDS Drive
Herndon, VA 22071
703/742-2000
Systems integrator. Offers Integrated Document Processing (IDP) service, a vendor-independent rewritable and WORM-based approach for capturing, storing, retrieving and publishing data; offers open architecture for Unix, VMS, DOS, and OS/2-based systems.

Electronic Trend Publications
12930 Saratoga Avenue, Suite D1
Saratoga, CA 95070
408/996-7416
Market research and analyses. *The Impact of Optical Technology on Paper, Microform and Magnetic Disk and Tape Storage* is a market research report.

ENDL Associates
29112 Country Hills Road
San Juan Capistrano, CA 92675
714/364-9626
Consulting organization owned by Ken Hallam (Chair of X3B11), the ANSI Technical Committee on Optical Media standardization) and I. Dal Allan (vice chair of X3T9.2, the ANSI Technological Committee on SCSI and ESDI). Publishes the *ENDL Letter*.

Energy Conversion Devices
1675 West Maple Road
Troy, MI 48084
313/280-1900
Developer of phase-change rewritable technology based on the structural re-arrangement of a thin film of material which stores information in a pattern of microscopic dots created by a laser. Technology being used by Matsushita.

Frame Technology Corporation
2911 Zanker Road
San Jose, CA 94134
408/433-3311
Uses the NeXT computer with Display Postscript.

Fuji Photo Film Co., Ltd.
Optical Memory Project
26-30, Nishiazabu 2-chome
Minato-ku, Tokyo 106, Japan

+81-406-2762
Developed 5.25-inch optical products including ablative and dye/polymer WORM as well as M-O rewritable media.

FWB, Inc.
2040 Polk Street, Suite 215
San Francisco, CA 94109
415/474-8055
Offers the hammerDisk600, a rewritable optical subsystem for Apple Macintosh network users for online backup data archiving applications. Uses the Ricoh 5.25-inch M-O rewritable drive.

Glaxo, Inc.
5 Moore Drive
Research Triangle Park, NC 27709
919/248-2100
Installed Alphatronix rewritable system to store physiologic data.

GoldStar
1130 East Arques Avenue
Sunnyvale, CA 94086
408/737-8575
Offers WORM as well as phase-change and rewritable 5.25-inch drives.

Gorham Advanced Materials Institute
POB 250
Gorham, ME 04038
207/892-5445
Thin Films for Electronic Optoelectronic and Optical Applications: Market Forecasts, Technology Assessments and New Business Opportunities to 1992 is a multi-client study.

Grenat Logiciel
6, Avenue des Andes, Bt. 4
Mini-Park, Z.I. Courtaboeuf,
91952 Les Ulis Cedex, France
33-1-64-46-45-54
STARFILE is a file management package for WORM disks and works on Sun IBM-PC/XT/AT, VAX, Prime, Norsk Data, VMS, Macintosh and Unix-based machines. STARFILE Erasable is based on the same principles for rewritable drives. Selected by European Space Agency for optical archiving of data from ERS 1 satellite.

GTX
8836 North 23rd Avenue
Phoenix, AZ
602/870-1696
Supplier of drawing conversion and management systems. The Drawing Management System incorporates LAN, mass storage devices, expert system techniques, raster and CAD vector processing. Engineering drawing system based on GTX 5000 raster to vector workstation using Shugart or Optimem WORM drives. Also offers rewritable system.

GTX, Ltd.
Farley Hall
London Road, Binfield
Bracknell, Berks RG12 5EU United Kingdom

Herstal Automation
3171 West Twelve Mile Road
Berkeley, MI 48072
313/548-2001
Developing optical subsystems based on Hewlett Packard 1000, 3000, 9000 series Unix workstations. These subsystems will feature Maxtor WORM and Ricoh rewritable 5.25-inch drives.

Hewlett-Packard
Greeley Storage Division
700 71st Avenue
Greeley, CO 80634
303/350-4580
The HP C171QA is an Optical Disk Library System, a rewritable optical disk autochanger using the Sony SMO-D501 5.25-inch rewritable drive and the SMO-C501, a SCSI host controller board. The HP Series 6300 Model 200GB/A library stores up to 20.8GB of data on 32 5.25-inch disks and uses the SCSI interface.

Hewlett-Packard
3000 Hanover Street
Palo Alto, CA 94304
415/857-1501
Research and development laboratory.

Hewlett-Packard U. K., Ltd.
Pinewood Information Systems Division

Nine Mile Ride
Wokingham, Berkshire
United Kingdom RG11 3LL
+44-344-763507

Hitachi America Ltd.
Computer Division
Hitachi Plaza
2000 Sierra Point Parkway
Brisbane, CA 9400
415/872-1902
Manufacturer of 5.25-inch rewritable optical disk drive, the OF112S SCSI formatter/controller, and WORM 12-inch drive and jukebox manufacturer.

Hitachi Sales Corporation
East Coast Office
Natick, MA 01760-1506
617/655-5501
Regional office.

Hitachi Europe, Ltd.
Trafalgar House
Hammersmith International Centre
2 Chalkhill Road
Hammersmith, London
United Kingdom W6
+44-81-748-2001

Hitachi-Maxell
12880 Moore Street
Cerritos, CA 90701
213/926-0916
WORM, rewritable and read-only optical media manufacturer.

Hoechst Celanese Corporation
Technology Development Optical Disk
One Main Street
Chatham, NJ 07928
201/635-4228
Ozadisc is the firm's 3.5- and 5.25-inch magneto-optic rewritable disk media and 5.25-inch dye-polymer WORM media. Joint venture with Nakamichi and KerDix to produce magneto-optic rewritable optical disks.

Hoechst
Rheingaustrasse 190
3540, D-6200 Wiesbaden 1
West Germany
+49-06134-206-0
Offers 3.5- and 5.25-inch M-O rewritable media.

IBM Japan Co., Ltd.
Decision Support System Marketing Division
3-2-12 Roppongi
Minato-Ku
Tokyo 108 Japan
+81-3-586-1111
Imagewide, an optical disk-based document management system connecting workstations via Token Ring LAN available only in Japan, uses Hitachi 5.25-inch rewritable drive and media.

IEM Inc.
POB 8915
Fort Collins, CO 80525
303/223-6071
Offers the 5365 subsystem using Sony 5.25-inch drive; SCSI and HP-18 interfaces are available

Image Business Systems Corporation
Two Grand Central Tower
New York, NY 10017
212/972-4400
800/YES-4.IBS
Spin-off of International Systems Services Company's document imaging business. Specializes in the integration of image processing into information systems. ImageSystem is a LAN-based document handling imaging application that runs on the IBM RT system under AIX. Signed cooperative marketing agreement with IBM who now owns a minority equity in the firm. Offers WORM and rewritable versions of ImageSystem, and optional Cygnet jukebox.

Institute for Computer Sciences & Technology
National Bureau of Standards
Technology Building, Room A61
Gaithersburg, MD

301/975-2947
Active in the establishment of standards for optical disk including the media testing.

International Data Corporation
Integrated Business Systems Services
5 Speen Street
Framingham, MA 01701
508/872-8200
Integrated Business Systems: Integrated Office Systems and Document Management" is an IDC Market Planning Service. The firm publishes market research studies and analyses in such areas as document image management systems, and optical storage.

International Information Management Congress (IMC)
345 Woodcliff Drive
Fairport, NY 14450
716/383-8330
Publisher of *IMC Journal* and sponsors Informatics and international conferences.

Jasmine
1740 Army Street
San Francisco, CA 94124
415/282-1111
DirectOptical is a 5.25-inch rewritable optical subsystem, based on the Ricoh engine and integrated with a Macintosh.

Kode
Division of Odetics, Inc.
1515 South Manchester
Anaheim, CA 92802-2907
714/758-0400
Time Interval Analyzers for measuring and testing bit shift and jitter in optical disk drives. Used by IBM, Eastman Kodak Company, Daicel, PDO, Cherokee, Optical Data, Panasonic, Sony, DEC, Maxtor, Verbatim, and others.

Kubota, Ltd.
Osaka, Japan
Entered into a joint venture with Maxtor to form Maxoptix Corporation based in San Jose, CA. Under this five-year agreement, Kubota will spend $12 million for a 25 percent equity share and obtain worldwide manufacturer rights and exclusive marketing rights.

Kyocera Co., Ltd.
Offers ANSI 3.5-inch M-O media for use in direct-overwrite drives as well as 5.25-inch M-O ISO-standard media.

Laserdrive, Ltd.
1101 Space Park Drive
Santa Clara, CA 95054
408/970-3600
Eastman Kodak and Olivetti purchase 80 percent of the company. Laserdrive has absorbed Verbatim's 3.5-inch TMO erasable optical drive and system development.

Linotype
425 Oser Avenue
Hauppauge, New York 11788
516/434-2000
OEM for Jasmine drive. Intends to market subsystem to publishing industry.

MACsetra Technologies International, Inc.
2237 York Avenue
Saskatoon, Saskatchewan
Canada AJ7 1H0
306/955-0022
The Genesis G6000 is a rewritable optical subsystem featuring Ricoh M-O rewritable drives and the Macintosh family of microcomputers including the IIcx, IIx, and SE/30.

Mass Optical Storage Technology, Inc. (M.O.S.T.)
23832 Rockfield Blvd., Suite 245
El Toro, CA 92630
714/583-2266
Introduced 3.5-inch M-O rewritable drive. Pinnacle Micro, Inc. is selling the system; Ocean Microsystems is offering the drive as Vista 130. M.O.S.T. is funded through Nakamichi.

Matsushita Electric Industrial Company
1006 Kadoma
Kadoma City
Osaka 571 Japan
06-908-1121
Recently announced the commercialization of a rewritable 3.5-inch 280MB optical disk in Japan using phase-change optical media. Firm offers optical

storage system designed for high-definition, digitally encoded images and uses 12-inch WORM phase-change disks. Offering 5.25-inch M-O subsystems — Seiko and Matsushita.

Maxcess, Inc.
314 North 13th Street, Suite 806
Philadelphia, PA 19108
215/928-1213
Offers 600L rewritable optical disk subsystem (using Sony M-O drive) for Macintosh.

Maxell Corporation
12880 Moore Street
Cerritos, CA 90701
213/926-0926
Offers WORM and rewritable (M-O) optical disk media and cartridges. The rewritable cartridges are designed for use in Hitachi's 5.25-inch rewritable optical drives.

Maxoptix Corporation
150 River Oaks
San Jose, CA 95134
408/432-1700
Joint venture of Maxtor and Kubota Ltd. (Japan) Maxtor transferred the technology and personnel for rewritable and WORM optical disk products to this joint venture. Focus on Tahiti 1, a 5.25-inch rewritable drive developed by Maxtor Corporation.

Maxtor Corporation
150 River Oaks Parkway
San Jose, CA 95134
408/432-1700
Discontinued Fiji 1, a 3.5-inch rewritable optical drive. Acquired systems integrator Storage Dimensions. The Tahiti I, a 5.25-inch 1GB drive has been repeatedly delayed. It claims a 35ms access time and thus is expected to serve as a primary storage device, replacing or complimenting a hard disk drive.

Meckler Corporation
11 Ferry Lane West
Westport, CT 06880
203/226-6967
Publishes bi-monthly *Optical Information Systems* journal which includes in-

depth articles and monthly *OIS Update* which focuses on current news about write-once and rewritable optical disk technology and application developments. Sponsors annual Document Image Automation Conference in the U.S. and OIS International in the U.K.

Meckler, Ltd.
Grosvenor Gardens House
Grosvenor Gardens
London SW1W 0BS United Kingdom
01-931-9985

Micro Design International, Inc.
6985 University Blvd.
Winter Park, FL 32792
407/677-8333
The LaserBank 600 R is a rewritable optical disk subsystem with software interfaces for MS-DOS, SCO XENIX or Novell NetWare operating systems. Subsystem uses Sony M-O drive. Offers a variety of software interfaces including the XENIX mountable and the LaserBank transparent.

Micro Dynamics, Ltd.
8555 Sixteenth Street, Suite 802
Silver Spring, MD 20910
301/589-6300
MARS is a Multi-user Archival Retrieval System that integrates the Calera Recognition System, Macintosh II, high-speed scanner, LAN, and ISi's 5.25-inch WORM drive. LSMI's and Sony 12-inch WORM drives are optional. New upgrades include jukeboxes, rewritable optical storage, and LAN software.

MicroNet Technology
20 Mason
Irvine, CA 92718
714/837-6033
Offers Sony M-O disk subsystem for IBM-PC/AT, PS/2 and compatible computers. When configured with a special device driver, the Micro/Optical system can "splice" two drives into one logical volume, giving customers access to 600MB of rewritable optical storage without having to turn over the disk.

Microtech International
158 Commerce Street
East Haven, CT 06512

203/468-6223
Offers OR650 rewritable optical storage system for Macintosh using Sony M-O drive.

Mirror Technologies
2644 Patton Road
Roseville, MN 55133
612/633-4450
The RM600 subsystem uses a 5.25-inch Sony M-O drive.

Mitsubishi Electronics America, Inc.
Computer Peripherals Division
991 Knox Street
Torrance, CA 90502
213/515-3993
5.25-inch WORM and rewritable drive and jukebox manufacturer.

Mitsubishi Kasei
5-2 Marunouchi 2-Chome
Chiyoda-Ku, Tokyo, Japan
+81-03-282-6760
Offers 5.25-inch WORM and 3.5- and 5.25-inch M-O rewritable optical media.

Mitsui Petrochemical
New Technology Development Center
Sodegaura, Chiba, Japan
Announced intention to manufacture 3.5-inch M-O media.

Morton Management, Inc.
12079 Tech Road
Silver Spring, MD 20904
301/622-5600
The GBMO subsystem uses a Ricoh 5.25-inch M-O drive.

National Institute of Standards and Technology (NIST)
Building 225-A61
Gaithersburg, MD 20899
301/975-2947
Sponsors Optical Media Research program for media testing and standardization.

NEC Corporation
33-1 Shiba 5-Chome

Minato-Ku
Tokyo 108, Japan
+81-3-452-8000
Offers a rewritable M-O subsystem using 3M media, ISO-standard drive with SCSI interface.

New Logic Research
1552 Beach Street
Oakland, CA
415/655-7305
Startup company developing polymer-dye rewritable media.

New York Life Insurance Comapny
51 Madison Avenue
New York, NY 1101
212/576-7778
End-user of AGA's WORM-based DISCUS. The information systems division is evaluating the NeXT Computer.

Next Technology Corporation, Ltd.
St. Johns Innovation Centre
Cambridge CB4 United Kingdom
+44-223-421-180
Voyager is jukebox capable of storing up to 180 5.25-inch rewritable disks.

NeXT, Inc.
3475 Deer Creek Road
Palo Alto, CA 94304
415/424-8500
Manufacturer of the NeXT workstation which uses the Canon erasable optical drive as its primary storage device. Offers NeXT lower-cost network user system that omits the M-O disk drive used in original workstation. All NeXT users have received a 40MB Quadram hard disk drive free of charge.

Software developers include Frame Technology and Lotus who reportedly plans to develop an advanced version of Lotus 1-2-3tm for NeXT's erasable optical drive.

N/Hance Systems, Inc.
908R Providence Highway
Dedham, MA 02026
617/461-1970; 800/BUY-WORM
Offers seven subsystems using Sony's rewritable optical disk drive.

North American Philips
100 East 42nd Street
New York, NY 10017
212/697-3600

Ocean Microsystems
246 East Hacienda Avenue
Campbell, CA 95008
800/262-3261
Offers 9650R Tidelwave subsystem using Sony M-O drive. The Vista 130 3.5-inch M-O drive meets the proposed ISO standard single-sided 128MB capacity. The drive is CAV and has a 28msec average seek time and a transfer rate of 512KBPs.

Oki Corporation
Hara Building, 7th Floor
4-11 Sakaecho
Takasaki City 370 Japan
+81-273-25-1525
Offering a 5.25-inch M-O rewritable drive that is a Ricoh OEM.

Olympus Corporation
Special Products Division
3000 Marcus Avenue, Suite 1E7
Lake Success, New York
516/488-3880
Developed rewritable optical disk SCSI subsystem.

Olympus Corporation
Technology Development Center
23456 Hawthorne Blvd., Suite 120
Torrance, CA
213/373-0696
MD-D501E is a 5.25-inch magneto-optical rewritable drive that uses 3M media. Developed a SCSI-based subsystem.

Olympus Optical Company GmbH
Wendenstrasse 14-16
D-2000 Hamburg 1
Federal Republic of Germany
49402-377-3168
Model ME-S5010E is a stand-alone 5.25-inch magneto-optic rewritable drive; the Model ME-D5010E is a built-in unit.

Optex Corporation
2 Research Court
Rockville, MD 20850
301/840-0011
Demonstrated that its electron trapping optical memory (ETOM) disk completed a 100 million read, write and erase cycle test without any material degradation or change in the physical characteristics of the media. The drive design was developed by Vision Three.

Optical Data, Inc.
9400 S.W. Gemini Drive
Beaverton, OR 97005
503/626-2211
Shut down in early 1990 after Tandy's announcement that it would introduce a commercial version of ODI's flexible rewritable optical media in its THOR-CD product line. Teijin, Ltd. is actively developing ODI's technology under license and expects to introduce commercial products. Developer of optical media including a flexible rewritable optical media.

Optical Storage Corporation
Minato-ku, Tokyo, Japan
Joint venture of Sumitomo Metal & Mining Co., Sumitomo Chemical Co., Ltd. and Daicel Chemical Industries, Ltd. to manufacture M-O media.

Optotech, Inc.
740 Wooten Road
Colorado Springs, CO 80915
303/570-7500
Key assets of Optotech were acquired by Hewlett-Packard at the end of 1989. Developing a 5.25-inch M-O rewritable drive.

Panasonic Communications and Systems Company
Two Panasonic Way
Secaucus, NJ 07094
800/742-8086
201/392-4603
Introduced multifunction (rewritable and write-once) 5.25-inch optical disk drive using direct overwrite phase-change optical storage technology.

Panasonic Deutschland GmbH
Neiderlassung, Munchen Bretonischer Ring 5
D-8011 Grasbrunn

West Germany
Offers the LF-9000S, a 5.25-inch M-O rewritable drive with a 326MB storage capacity per disk side.

Pegasus Disk Technologies
55 Crest Avenue
Walnut Creek, CA 94595
415/938-3345
415/439-7845
WORM and rewritable optical drive and jukebox integration firm. specializes in Sony network compatible jukeboxes.

Pentax Teknologies
880 Interlocken Parkway
Broomfield, CO 80020
303/460-1600
Manufacturer of 5.25-inch WORM and magneto-optic heads. The Optical Head and Media Tester can be used for WORM, CD, LaserVision, and M-O rewritable drives.

Perceptive Solutions, Inc.
1509 Falcom, Suite 104
DeSoto, TX 75115
214/224-6774
Offers the hyperSTORE, a one-controller solution to applications that utilize a variety of mass storage devices including rewritable optical disk drives and floppies.

Peripheral Land, Inc.
47421 Bayside Parkway
Fremont, CA 94538
415/657-2211
Offers Infinity Optical rewritable storage subsystem for IBM-PC/AT/XT and PS/2 computers as well as Macintosh using Sony M-O drive. Comes in single or double-drive configurations and bundled with an extensive collection of utility software: TurboBack, TurboCache, TurboOptizimer, and ACE! from Casady and Green, Inc., a security software package for the Macintosh.

Philips and Du Pont Optical
1409 Foulk Road
Wilmington, DE 19803
302/479-2507

Offers 12-inch and 5.25-inch magneto-optic (M-O) rewritable optical disk media which will be used with Maxtor's Tahiti 1 drive. Manufactures rewritable optical disks at its Kings Mountain, North Carolina plant.

Philips Business Systems
Elektra House
Bergholt Road
Colchester
Essex CO4 5BE United Kingdom
0206-575115
Drive and media manufacturer.

Philips Research Laboratories
Building WY 7
5600 JA Eindhoven
The Netherlands
31-40-742424
Reported promising group of rewritable optical materials such as gallium antimonide and indium antimonide using phase change techniques for the recording of analog and digital signals. Materials will not be used into new products in the near term.

Pinnacle Micro
15265 Alton Parkway
Irvine, CA 92718
800/553-7070
714/727-3300
Implemented Sony M-O drive, the SMO-S501, in a Macintosh computer environments. The REO-650 is a single drive, SCSI system; the REO-1300 is a dual drive subsystem. Software supports a host of working environments: UNIX, Xenix, Novell and Netware 2.1.

Engineered a Macintosh-compatible 16GB erasable optical disk jukebox (REO-16000) which is being distributed by Ingram Micro D Inc. Also sells M.O.S.T.'s 3.5-inch M-O drive.

Pioneer Electric Corporation
4-1 Meguro 1-Chome
Meguro-ku
Tokyo 153 Japan
+81-3-495-9808
Offers 5.25-inch rewritable/write-once multifunction optical disk drive.

Pioneer Communications of America, Inc.
600 East Crescent Avenue
Upper Saddle River, NJ 07458
201/327-6400
Pioneer's multifunction optical disk drive will also be sold by Optimem, and Laser Magnetic Storage International (LMSI).

Procom Technology, Inc.
200 McCormick Avenue
Costa Mesa, CA 92626
714/549-9449
Offers the MEOD650/E, a SCSI rewritable disk drive manufactured by Sony for IBM-PC/AT/XT; the MCD-ROM 650 is for the Macintosh.

RACET Computes, Ltd.
3150 East Birch Street
Brea, CA 92621
714/579-1725
The COSMOS 600 M-O is a standalone rewritable optical subsystem compatible with IBM compatibles and Macintosh and uses Sony M-O drive.

Relax Technology
3101 Whipple Road, Suite 22
Union City, CA 94587
415/471-6112
Offers rewritable optical disk subsystem using Ricoh M-O drive for Macintosh, Sun or IBM-PCs.

Remark Associates
431 Clipper Street
San Francisco, CA 94114
415/641-6033
Principal is Les Cowan, former editor of *Optical Memory News*. Consulting firm devoted to the development and utilization of optical storage technologies.

Ricoh Corporation
3001 Orchard Parkway
San Jose, CA 95134
408/432-8800
WORM and rewritable optical disk drive manufacturer. The RO-5030E is a 5.25-inch rewritable optical drive. Also offers a "dual function" (multifunction) write-once/rewritable optical disk drive.

Ricoh Deutschland GmbH
Data Processing Section
Mergenthaler Allee 38-40
6236 Eschborn 1
Federal Republic of Germany
0-6196-906-0

Ricoh Europe
Dusseldorf Branch
Hansaalle 201
4000 Dusseldorf 11
Federal Republic of Germany
49-0-211-5285-0

Ricoh UK, Ltd.
Ricoh House
2 Plane Tree Crescent
Feltham, Middlesex
TW13 7HG United Kingdom
01-751-6611

Ricoh Corporation
2-38-5 Nishi Shimbashi
Minatuo-ku
Tokyo 105 Japan
+81-3-578-3111

Rothchild Consultants
256 Laguna Honda Blvd.
San Francisco, CA 94116-1496
415/681-3700
Optical memory marketing and technology consulting services offered worldwide. Publications include *Optical Memory News*, and the *Optical Memory Report.* The firm offers a continuing information service, Optical System Information Service, and sponsors the Technology Opportunity Conferences.

SKC, Ltd.
460 Chon Hung-Ri
Chonan
Chungchongnam-do 333-830
Korea
+82-417-568-4221

Intends to manufacture ISO-standard 5.25-inch M-O media for the Sony M-O 5.25-inch rewritable drive.

Seiko Epson
Suwa Minami
Japan
Offers 5.25-inch M-O media with a plastic substrate; engineering for use with the Sony 5.25-inch M-O drive.

Semi-Tech Microelectronics
131 McNabb Street
Markham, Ontario
L3R 5V7 Canada
Developing a low-end 5.25-inch M-O rewritable optical drive and media.

Sharp Electronics Corporation
10 Sharp Plaza
Mahway, NJ 07430-2135
201/529-8200
Model JY-500 is a 5.25-inch rewritable magneto-optic drive and media. Demonstrated computer color imaging system that uses a color scanner, color thermal transfer printer and Model JY-500.

Sony Corporation of America
Optical Storage Technology
Sony Drive
Park Ridge, NJ 07656
201/930-6025
5.25- and 3.5-inch M-O rewritable drive and media manufacturer.

Sony Microsystems Company
1049 Elwell Court
Palo Alto, CA 94303
415/965-4492
Offers high-performance workstations that can be configured with rewritable optical storage.

SPIE (International Society for Optical Engineers)
POB 10
Bellingham, WA 98227-0010

206/676-3290
Professional organization that publishes include *Optical Engineering* journal, and *Optical Engineering Reports*, and sponsors conferences.

Specialized Systems Technology, Inc.
POB 420489
Houston, TX 77242-0489
713/781-8993
The DOM 650 subsystem uses a Ricoh M-O drive.

Storage Dimensions
2145 Hamilton Avenue
San Jose, CA 95125
408/879-0300
Subsidiary of Maxtor Corporation. The firm has demonstrated the Tahiti 1 rewritable drive with an IBM-PC/AT. LaserStor is a 5.25-inch optical subsystem for IBM-PC, IBM PS/2, and Macintosh environments with Ricoh/Maxtor WORM and rewritable drives. LaserCache is a software package. Storage Dimensions owns the rights to Tallgrass Technologies LightFile product line.

StoragePlus, Inc. (formerly Sumo Systems)
1580 Old Oakland Road
Suite C-103
San Jose, CA 95131
408/286-5744
Markets a rewritable optical subsystem, the RSSM600-C series, using the Ricoh M-O rewritable drive for the Macintosh. The firm also supplies a host adapter for the IBM-PC and compatibles.

Summus Computer Systems
17171 Park Row, Suite 300
Houston, TX 77084
713/578-3303
Offers LightDisk 650 rewritable subsystem for Macintosh, DEC and Q-Bus and Unibus computers, Sun workstations and IBM-PC/AT and compatibles using Sony M-O drive.

Sunstone, Inc.
POB 807
Plainsboro, NJ 08536
609/452-9523
Research, development, and manufacturer of rewritable optical media based on infrared phosphors.

SuperMac Technology
4805 Potrero Avenue
Sunnyvale, CA 94086
408/245-2202
Based on Sony M-O drive, the firm offers the DataFrame RS Optical Drive.

Symmetrical Technologies, Inc. (Symtech)
301 Gallaher View Road, Suite 231
Knoxville, TN 37919
615/690-3838
Offers the M.O.S.T. rewritable optical subsystem for Sun workstations, Macintosh and DEC VAX computers. M.O.S.T. is an acronym for Magneto-optic storage technology and is based on the Sony M-O drive.

Tandy THOR-CD Technologies
1300 One Tandy Center
Fort Worth, TX 76102
817/390-3693
Announced rewritable compact optical disk media and drive system, THOR-CD™ (THOR stands for Tandy High-intensity Optical Recording) based on Optical Data, Inc.'s technology. Media to play on a standard CD audio player. In 1990, Tandy announced an indefinite delay beyond a 1991 target date for the introduction of THOR-CD. Development will focus on a consumer audio version of THOR.

Tecmar
6225 Cochran Road
Solon, OH 44139-3377
216/349-0600
The LaserVault is a subsysstem using a Sony's 650MB rewritable optical disk drive.

Teijin, Ltd.
Exploratory Research Laboratory
Tokyo Research Center
4-3-2, Asahigaoka Hino
Tokyo, 191 Japan
Purchased license of ODI's flexible rewritable optical media and is currently working on commercialization of the media.

Ten X Technology, Inc.
4807 Spicewood Springs Road
Building 3, Suite 3200
Austin, TX 78759

800/922-9050
512/346-8360
The Opti Xchange is a subsystem that includes the Pioneer 5.25-inch multi-function (rewritable/write-once) drive with a SCSI interface.

Toshiba Coproration
1-1-1 Shibaura
Minato-ku
Tokyo 105 Japan
+81-3-457-2725
Offers 5.25-inch rewritable M-O disk drive.

Toshiba America Information Systems, Inc.
9740 Irvine Blvd
Irvine, CA 92718
714/583-3084
Offering model (Tosfile 550SD-4R) of Tosfile electronic document filing system using Toshiba's 5.25-inch M-O drive which does not conform to ISO standards.

Tosoh USA, Inc.
Subsidiary of Tosoh Company (Japan)
800 C Gateway Blvd
South San Francisco, CA 94080
415/588-5200
Offers magneto-optical media for 5.25- and 3.5-inch optical disk drives; also offers continuous servo and sample servo formats.

Trimarc Systems, Inc.
14100 Laurel Park Drive, Suite D
Laurel, MD 20707
301/792-8600
EMA Color 1000, an image handling system that incorporates their scanner product line, uses a Sony 5.25-inch M-O drive; it is for the IBM-PC and Apple Macintosh platforms.

Trimarchi
POB 560
State College, PA 16804
814/234-.5659
The Equalizer series offer Las-er-ase, a rewritable optical disk drives to Microvax 2000 users. Configuration uses either Sony or Ricoh 5.25-inch M-O rewritable drives.

The Datakeg Twin Sixes optical disk drives for DEC, Sun, Macintosh and IBM-PC users. Dual drives offer Winchester technology and provide rewritable optical storage as a backup.

Tristar Technology, Inc.
10 Reuten Drive
Closter, NJ 07624
210/784-1557
Offers four Ricoh M-O rewritable optical disk drive-based subsystems: PE3660-1D, PE3660-1DQm, PE3600-1R, and PE3660-2R.

U.S. Design Corporation
A Maxtor Company
4311 Forbes Blvd.
Lanham, MD 20706
301/577-2880
Expanded the firm's Q-Stor family of storage systems to include Sony rewritable optical drives for DEC and Sun platforms. Systems integrator for DEC and Sun computers. Software products include JukeVOX for the Sony jukebox.

University of Iowa
Weeg Computing Center
Lindquist Hall, Room 229
Iowa City, IA 52242
319/335-5470
Developed a WORM-based system for storing medical images for purposes of medical education. WORM and rewritable end-user.

Verbatim Corporation
Subsidiary of Eastman Kodak Company
1200 W. T. Harris Blvd.
Charlotte, NC 28213
704/547-6500
Opened media manufacturing operation for 14-inch WORM disks. Signed joint venture agreement with Mitsubishi to market Verbatim's 3.5-inch magneto-optic rewritable optical disks in Japan.

University of Washington
Hospital Center
Seattle, WA
206/548-6725
Imaging application using Jasmine DirectOptical Macintosh-based subsystem.

Western Digital Corporation
2445 McCabe Way
Irvine, CA 92714
714/863-0102
WDATXT-FASST is a SCSI host bus adapter kit for the connection of WORM, rewritable and CD-ROM drives and other peripherals to IBM-PC and compatible computers.

XYXIS Corporation
7084 Shady Oak Road
Eden Prairie, MN 55344
612/944-8288
Offers the XY600RW series of rewritable optical storage subsystems (based on the Ricoh M-O drive) for Sun, Macintosh and IBM and compatible microcomputers.

Zetaco Corporation
6850 Shady Oak Road
Eden Prairie, MN 55344
612/941-9480
The Model SKR-600 is a 5.25-inch 594MB rewritable subsystem compatible with Data General's MV Series of minicomputers.

References

1. See Geoffrey Russell's chapter on the development of flexible rewritable optical media for an in-depth technical description and discussion of ODI's media.

2. Certain substances, when exposed to a magnetic field, will rotate the plane of polarization of light reflected from them. This phase-change is called the Kerr effect.

3. All references in this chapter may be found in Appendix A: Recommended Readings.

2
Rewriting the Future: Rewritable Optical Mass Storage Comes of Age

Robert B. Mueller

Gone are the days when an engineer using CAD/CAE (computer-aided design/computer-aided engineering) applications could speak comfortably of the distinctions between mini- and microcomputers. The advent of 32-bit processors delivers computing power to the desktop once associated with larger and more expensive workstations. Today, architects and engineers can run sophisticated three-dimensional (3-D), solids modeling, shading, simulations, and structural analysis applications on inexpensive DOS- or Unix-based workstations costing less than $15,000.

However, the one critical feature separating established minicomputers from microcomputers has been mass storage capacity. CAD/CAE applications are gluttons for memory. CAD/CAE drawings are large data files, and system designers require considerable mass storage capacity for scanned images, design iterations, related attributable databases, and technical documentation.

To cope with the mass storage crisis, engineers were forced to carve up large or very detailed drawings into smaller drawings lined by pointers, resulting in awkward, jury-rigged, complex storage and filing. Online access to reference materials was minimal or nonexistent. File transfer via network was tediously slow and cumbersome when data and/or image files could be transferred at all. Additional iterations became more a problem to be avoided rather than an opportunity to perfect a design.

In 1990, engineers benefited from a major technological breakthrough: rewritable optical information storage. In the fall of 1990, rewritable optical storage celebrated its first birthday as a commercially available mass storage technology. The leading form of rewritable optical storage available today is magneto-optical (M-O), which combines magnetic and laser technologies to accomplish the tasks of reading, writing, and erasing, and rewriting of information.

Sony Corporation's 5.25-inch Full-Height Magneto-Optical Rewritable Optical Disk Drives. (Courtesy, Sony Corporation of America)

How Optical Storage Works

Optical storage uses a laser beam focused to a tiny spot to write data on a disk, tape or plastic card. On a rewritable optical disk, data are written magnetically. In other forms of optical storage, actual physical marks are made. In both cases, because the laser spot on the disk is so small — a micron or less in diameter — data can be packed far more densely than on a magnetic disk or tape. A micron is one millionth of a meter. Approximately one hundred million of the marks made on an optical disk would fit on a fingernail — give or take a few million. This dense packing of marks or magnetic domains, which we refer to as high data density, makes it possible to achieve large storage capacity.

The small marks alone are not sufficient researchers discovered when they began developing optical storage in the 1960s. The smaller the marks, the harder it is to keep a drive head positioned directly over them, especially on a spinning disk. The head is the interface between the physical marks on a disk and the electronics that convert those marks into a signal that carries digital data. The head reflects a laser beam off the disk in order to read the marks on it, and if the disk is writable, the head shoots a laser beam at the disk to make the marks in the first place.

An optical head consists of a tiny diode laser, a lens, mirrors and other optical components, and devices called actuators which move the head in three directions. Tracks on the disk are spaced a microscopic 1.6 microns apart, and the head must be moved back and forth laterally to keep the head the proper distance above the disk, so that the laser beam stays in focus on the disk surface. Finally, there are still other actuators that constantly move the head slightly forward and backward, linearly along the track, so that the drive stays synchronized with the marks moving past the head, as the disk spins — at speeds ranging from about 200 RPM in the case of the inner tracks of a CD-ROM disc to about 3,000 RPM for the fastest commercial optical drives.

The dimensions are so small and the movements so fast, that the are unimaginable in terms of direct experience. If the whole apparatus were scaled up to more familiar dimensions, however, an average optical drive reading a disk would be the equivalent of a Boeing 747 cruising at an altitude of three miles, from which it never varies by more than 12 feet as it accurately follows a flight line 16 feet wide, at an unvarying speed of 123 million miles per hour.

Optical disks are removable for two reasons. First, the head flies-inch more than a millimeter above the disk surface, leaving ample rom to insert or eject a disk without the obstruction by the head. Second, the recording material in a disk is not on the surface. Instead, it is covered by a relatively thick protective coating. As a result, the laser beam, which is focused on the recording material, is out of focus at the surface of the disk. Therefore, any dirt, dust or scratches on the surface will also be out of focus, and will not affect the working of the laser beam. Normal amounts of foreign material, such as dust, make no difference, so the disk need not be sealed in an airtight chamber, like a fixed magnetic disk.

Beyond these basic elements common to all optical disks, each type of disk is the result of specific technical breakthroughs achieved by its developers.

Rewritable Optical Storage

The majority of today's M-O systems are based upon a two-sided 5.25-inch optical disk with up to 650MBs of storage (over 300MBs per disk side). The rewritable M-O optical disk is composed of two 10-nanometer-thick magnetic recording layers pressed between two polycarbonate layers.

It took years of laboratory research to produce today's efficient and long-lasting thin film recording materials which are most often alloys of terbium, iron, cobalt and traces of other elements. The proportion of each ele-

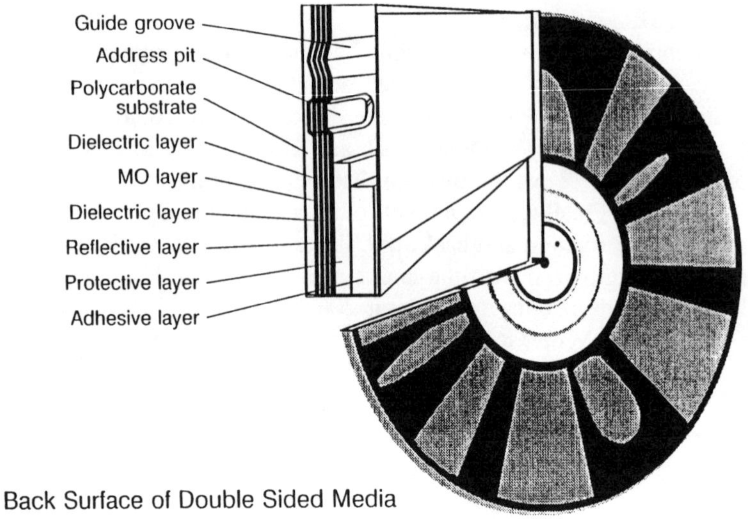

Figure 1. Structure of Magneto-Optical Disk. (Courtesy, Sony Corporation of America)

ment is adjusted to tune the medium to a certain temperature, called a Curie temperature, at which its magnetic coercivity drops to near zero. This simply means that it can be magnetized by a low power, ambient magnetic field, called a bias field. At any temperature other than the Curie temperature, the medium is unaffected by any magnetic field, no matter how strong. The Curie temperature of an M-O disk is typically around 180 degrees Centigrade (356 degrees Fahrenheit), so under normal conditions there is no danger of accidentally erasing an M-O disk, as there is with a floppy.

The M-O recording process is quite similar to conventional magnetic storage. Digital information is written on the disk's magnetic layer as a series of flux reversals. The polarity of each bit is either a north-pole down (representing digital), or a north-pole-up (digital 1).

Changing the bit's magnetic direction is an optical process. Regular magnets are not sufficiently powerful to switch the bit orientation, and stronger magnets would affect other bits on the disk. To reverse the bit's polarity without affecting other data, the M-O disk drive's laser beam heats the surface above the bit for approximately 800 nanoseconds to the magnetic film's Curie point of 150 degrees C. The film's magnetic properties are transformed at this temperature, thus allowing the drive's magnet to alter the direction of the bit. The laser beam pulses on and off while the disk rotates in the drive. If the laser is instructed to turn on when the magnet is polarized north-pole-up, the drive writes digital 1's; digital O's are written when the

Principle of Writing

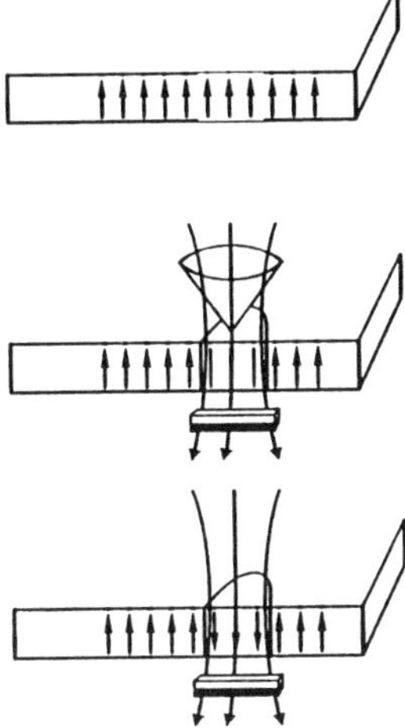

Figure 2a. Principles of Writing and Erasing. (Courtesy, Sony Corporation of America) A weak biasing magnetic field is applied to the disk which has been premagnetized in one direction on the perpendicular axis.

magnet is north-pole-down and the laser is on. If the laser is off, the information remains the same.

The head of a magneto-optic drive includes a small magnet, which supplies the bias field. The magnet's field can be switched between positive and negative by using either a switchable electro-magnet or by turning a physical magnet. When the laser beam heats a tiny spot on the disk to the Curie temperature, the spot becomes magnetized to the polarity of the bias field: positive if the field is switched positive at that moment; negative if it is negative.

Reading the magnetized spots on the disk involves a principle of physics known as the Kerr effect. The Kerr effect occurs because when the laser beam strikes the bit, the polarization of the bit makes the reflected beam rotate either clockwise or counterclockwise, depending upon the bit's magnetic direction. By sensing the direction of the beam rotation, the drive can determine if the bit is a digital.

Rewriting is a simple matter of returning a sector to its original polarity and then writing over it. Today's magneto-optic media have been tested through more than one million rewrites with no degradation in performance or data reliability.

Principle of Erasing

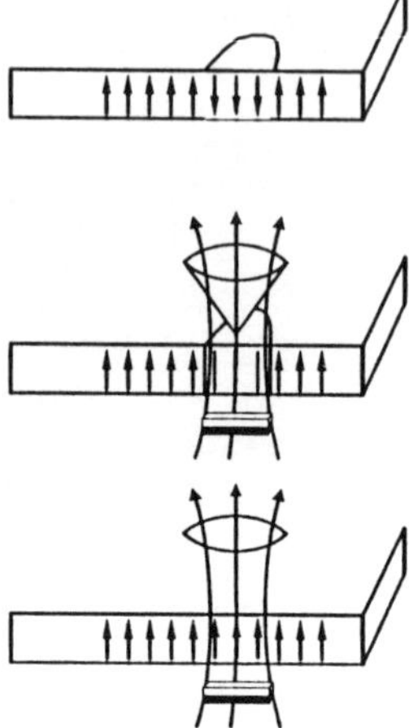

Figure 2b. Principles of Writing and Erasing. (Courtesy, Sony Corporation of America) A laser rapidly heats a spot on the disk; when the temperature of magneto-optical layer reaches its Curie point, it changes magnetic orientation as determined by the biasing magnetic field. After the laser beam is removed, the exposed disk region returns to a normal temperature and a magnetic spot remains.

In order to rewrite on the M-O disk, the drive performs a dual-pass operation. The initial pass is to erase existing information, a process accomplished by reversing the magnet's polarity and turning on the laser for one disk rotation. All areas of the disk selected for revised data become digital Os. In the second, or rewrite pass, the polarity is again switched, the laser is turned on for a rotation, and digital Is are written in the appropriate locations.

Features and Characteristics of Rewritable Optical Storage

Using proven magneto-optical technology, companies like the Sony Corporation are offering affordable removable rewritable optical disks with 650MBs of storage capacity that can be used over and over again. Not only do these rewritable optical disks deliver more storage space than most large-capacity Winchester hard disks, they also have a longer life and higher degree of reliability than hard disks, tape, or floppy diskettes. Additionally, rewritable optical disks offer far greater storage convenience and information access than aperture cards for a variety of applications.

For microcomputer-based CAD/CAE users, rewritable optical storage offers five distinct advantages over other storage media:

1. Cost-effectiveness
2. Increased memory capacity
3. Rewritability
4. Removability
5. Data security

Cost-Effectiveness

A typical CAD/CAE drawing is between 400KBs and 400MBs in size. When attribute files for numerous drawings in a design project are considered as well, it is typical for a complete project to use 100 to 200MBs of optical disk space.

Magnetic hard disks suitable for CAD/CAE applications have an average cost of $30 per megabyte. Furthermore, they must serve both as storage for application software, current work files, and iteration or historical files. Moreover it is typical for an engineer to have online reference materials, training programs, online help, or utility applications.

Given the cost-per-megabyte, magnetic hard disks are not cost-effective storage media in most CAD/CAE applications. Additionally, since hard disks are not removable, backup, restore and data distribution operations are cum-

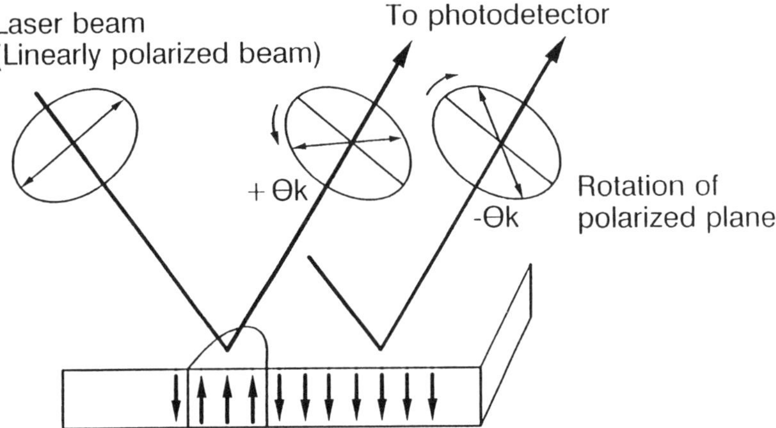

Figure 3. Principle of Reading. (Courtesy, Sony Corporation of America) A linearly polarized weak laser beam is focused on the disk's recording layer. Due to the Kerr effect, the plane of polarization of the reflected beam rotates clockwise or counterclockwise according to the magnetization in the recording layer pointing up or down. After passing through a polarization analyzer, the light strikes a photodetector where changes in light intensity are interpreted as binary data.

bersome, at best. At worst, they can be an often neglected annoyance involving tape mounts or keeping track of several floppy diskettes. Floppies and nine-track tape both cost around $2 per megabyte at their highest capacities which is approximately six times more than rewritable optical disk. Floppy diskette and magnetic tapes are also not particularly well-suited for storing the CAD/CAE drawings. Even a 1.4MBs double-sided, double-density floppy diskette is insufficient for storing CAD/CAE images. Since magnetic tapes are sequential access devices, they are too slow for use in distribution applications. Optical disks are random access devices that provide rapid data retrieval for online use.

Thus, from a price/performance perspective, rewritable optical devices provide the most cost-effective storage available for the CAD/CAE workstation user. A Sony 5.25-inch rewritable optical disk cartridge costs about 37 cents per-megabyte. This low-cost, coupled with the cartridge's removability, makes rewritable optical disks the most cost-effective device to handle virtually all of a computer system's mass storage tasks.

Storage Capacity

Another advantage of optical disks is their large storage capacity which conveys benefits beyond just allowing more information to be stored on a single removable medium. First-generation optical disks are not a replacement for DASD intensive magnetic storage. However, they are a completely new level in the storage hierarchy that allows for new applications and types of information to be managed. This means that optical storage, far from outdating the use of magnetic disks, will make magnetic disks more effective by freeing them of the burden of storing extremely large data and image files.

The large capacity of optical disks will allow the integration of multiple data types into applications. For example, optical disks are large enough to store digital video information. As new compression technologies, such as Intel Corporation's DVI (Digital Video Interactive) for video compression, come to market within the next few years, optical storage will emerge as the storage medium of choice for digital data of all types.

Why is this important to the CAD/CAE designer? Images are memory-intensive: a digitally-scanned photo consumes a minimum of one megabyte. Increasingly, engineers are integrating video images into design databases for more accurate representation of the constructed environment, simulation, animation, and presentation. The popularity of AutoDesk's new Animator program can be attributed to the use of images once associated with video now becoming an integral part of the CAD/CAE designer's world.

Finally, cost-effective rewritable optical mass storage solves a problem that has challenged engineers who use "imperfect" software solutions to convert raster fields to vector, and vice versa. Optical disks provide so much storage that both vector and raster files can be kept, each applied to the uses it supports best: vector for smooth, scaled outlines, and raster for solids modelling and larger color surfaces.

Rewritability

Since the recording method of a rewritable optical disk is magneto-optical, a sector can be erased and rewritten more than a million times with no degradation of the data according to accelerated life cycle tests in the laboratory. This is an advantage that distinguishes it from other optical mass storage technologies, such as WORM (Write-Once, Read-Many) and CD-ROM.

Rewritability has several advantages in engineering application. As previously noted, CAD/CAE drawings are typically developed through multiple iterations. A base drawing is copied a number of times. Each copy is developed according to a different approach until the best approach emerges. For example, design drawings for submarines for the British Navy go through approximately twenty iterations. However, once the best drawing is chosen, the others are of no further use. Rewritability allows reclamation of the disk space holding any drawings.

Rewritability also has advantages in backup and restore operations. Rewritable optical storage, both drive subsystems and jukeboxes, will be useful as network servers, especially as high-bandwidth fiber optic-based systems eliminate the throughput constraints that currently limit networks.

Removability

A disk that can be removed from its' drive is far more versatile than a fixed disk. Rewritable optical disks allow users to easily transport large amounts of data between high- and low-end workstations. This type of transportable storage capacity, uneconomical with magnetic disks, allows all of a company's work to be continuously available to all its designers. For example, template designs can be re-used indefinitely, and the company's bottom line would subsequently benefit from leveraged re-use of design details.

The raster side of CAD/CAE (growing in importance) would also benefit. Raster bit-mapped versions of drawing are either converted from vector drawing or scanned. Two thousand C-size drawings can be compressed and stored on a single 5.25-inch rewritable optical disk. Each drawing can be indexed into a database for quick access and display. In addition, each drawing can be revised since the medium is rewritable.

This kind of system permits drawings for entire projects to be stored on a single disk. For example, all information used to submit a government bid could be submitted on a single 5.25-inch rewritable optical disk rather than on aperture cards. Indeed, an increasing number of government agencies are switching over, or planning to move away from aperture cards, to optical disk.

Using a rewritable optical disk as a central store for scanned or otherwise rasterized drawings would also result in better control of vital management information. An engineering project is greater than the drawings: an organization must be able to maintain volumes of technical documentation, government rules and regulations, and vital internal correspondence that traces the evolution of the program. Currently, the average access to a paper drawing can take two days when located at all. Moreover, matching the image with the relevant text and data can be a nightmare. If all parts of a project are stored centrally, it is considerably easier to access and manipulate the information.

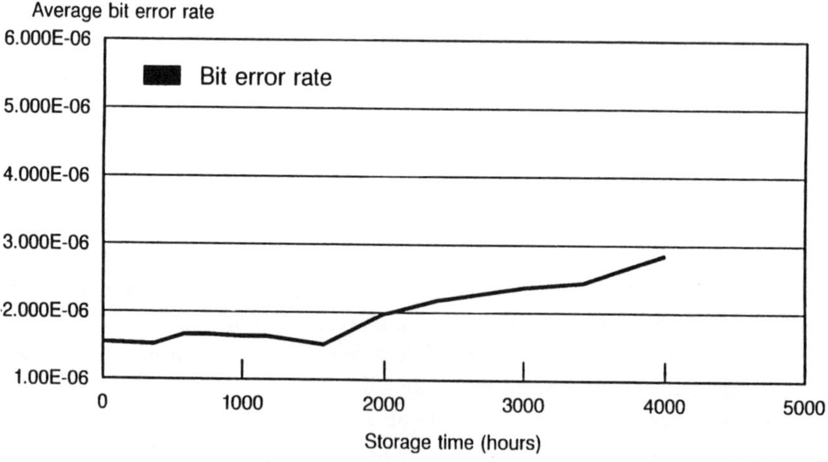

Figure 4. Insert Accelerated Life Test Table. (Courtesy, Sony Corporation of America) Based on accelerated test results obtained under conditions of 80 degrees centigrade and 85 percent relative humidity, Sony's rewritable optical media is expected to exhibit no substantial increase in error rate for a period of more than one hundred years in a normal office environment (Sony test results).

Data Security and Permanence

Both optical disk and tape technology provides one of the most secure forms of information storage. The most secure technology is WORM which transforms the media so that no information can be altered and remove. In addition, write-once optical media has an especially long life; for example, Sony's Century Media™ has a projected lifespan of 100 years based upon acceleration tests conducted in the laboratory.

Therefore, if ensuring data integrity is a concern, especially in cases of irreplaceable or difficult to locate information, or if a secure audit trail must be established, WORM optical media is the most appropriate solution. However, many of the same characteristics associated with WORM are also applicable to rewritable with a few additional advantages as well.

First, rewritable optical media has a projected media life of ten to fifteen years which is most probably a conservative estimate. This period may be sufficient for most users. Also, the 5.25-inch optical disk format with 650MBs storage capacity makes rewritable optical disk easy to remove and place in a small office safe or other secure location; it is not as easy to manipulate 12-inch WORM platters.

Another form of security is secondary storage. Companies including Hewlett-Packard are using rewritable optical disk to backup and archive data stored on the system's primary storage devices. Called DASS (Direct Access Secondary Storage) rewritable optical disk is also being used to log transactions, interchange data between systems and users, distribute software, and perform automatic backups without operator intervention.

Rewritable optical storage makes sense for DASS applications because it strikes a necessary balance between storage costs and performance capabilities. According to Hewlett-Packard, the average access time for hard disks is measured in tens of milliseconds (typically, a hard disk has an access time of under 30 ms). Access time for information on magnetic tapes is measured in tens of seconds for a mounted tape and minutes to hours for a tape in an automated library. The cost of magnetic disk storage is about $15 to $30 per megabyte whereas the cost of tape storage is 15¢ to 20¢ per megabyte.

With an average access time in the .1 to 10 second range, and a cost of twenty-cents to forty-cents per megabyte, rewritable optical drives are creating a new layer in the storage hierarchy.

Multiplying Future Productivity Through Optical Storage

The information age has introduced an environment in which microelectronic devices can conduct a dialogue, send pictures through the galaxy, instantly perform calculations that used to take weeks, capture three-dimensional images of the insides of our bodies and play music with lasers. A critical step in enhancing these achievements is the development of mass storage.

Mass storage usually refers to devices such as external disk drives, tape systems and other media than can statically hold more information than fits inside a computer's microchip memory (RAM). Spreadsheets, multiple page documents, engineering drawings, catalogs of parts, databases of customer records are all too big for RAM. Until recently, bulky records were too big for computer storage and were stored on paper or microfiche/microfilm.

Information can be retrieved from RAM nearly instantaneously, but RAM is expensive. Mass storage is much less expensive but slower than RAM. Today's mass storage media, in ascending order of capacity, include magnetic media such as floppy disks, tape and hard disks, as well as the newest form of mass storage media, the optical disk. The optical disk has more storage capacity, greater versatility and lower cost than any previous storage device.

Mass storage has always been one of the few fundamental elements in any computer system along with processors, RAM, and input/output devices such as the mouse, keyboards, printers and displays. Because mass storage is so essential to any computer system, an increase in its capabilities broadens the usefulness of computers and the productivity of their users. A single optical disk is now being used to store the voice of an expert mechanic, a set of engineering drawings and video footage of the component being repaired. An individual's medical records can now be carried on an optical memory card or disk that fits easily in a shirt pocket.

Computers, and electronic devices of all kind, process and transmit, capture and recombine, synthesize, display and sort data. When data are processed intelligently, the product is information which enhances analysis, planning and decision making.

Storage capacity eventually places a limit on the amount of information available. Increased capacity of mass storage devices makes it possible to accomplish bigger tasks as well as new and different ones.

There will be a profound effect on the way institutions acquire, process and disseminate information. Schools use information to stimulate the intellect. Governments use information to stimulate the economy, maintain order and administer justice. Business uses information to design products and to serve markets. Institutions strive to process and disseminate information at the highest possible speeds. However the amount of information available can become so large that organizing and processing it is an increasingly enormous challenge.

James Burke, a philosopher who examines the role of science in human affairs, emphasizes that throughout history, whenever new information technologies have radically altered the amount of information available, existing institutions have been reorganized into more complex forms.

Optical storage is such a technology. It is already beginning to change our lives and our institutions. In the near future, businesses, schools, governments and homes may become unrecognizable in the ways they communicate, both internally and with each other, in the complexity of their structure and in the scope of their responsibilities.

The Benefits of Optical Storage

Optical disks have three characteristics responsible for their advantages over other kinds of mass storage: very large storage capacities, removability, ability to access multiple disks per drive, and rapid access to information. The large storage capacities and removability result from the use of a laser instead of a magnetic field to make marks on the medium. Of course, fast access is characteristic of both magnetic and optical disks.

The significance of these characteristics is that a compact disc can store several encyclopedias. One rewritable optical disk with the same diameter as a floppy diskette can store the equivalent of 650 floppy diskettes. A 12-inch WORM optical disk can store the images of more than 70,000 typical office documents. Like optical disks, tape has large storage capacities and is removable; however, tape access is linear whereas disk access is random.

Fixed magnetic disks, such as a hard disk in a microcomputer, have large storage capacities. The largest hold up to several million bytes, but magnetic hard disks cannot be removed from the drive, and on a dollar-per-byte basis, they are much more expensive than optical disks. Floppy diskettes are removable, but with a capacity of about one million bytes of data, the equivalent of about 600 typed, double-spaced pages, they don't offer very large amounts of storage space. Even though this capacity is currently being increased, it can never even begin to match that of the optical disk.

Removability provides security, interchangeability and flexibility. At the end of the day, a disk can simply be taken out of its drive and locked up. Interchangeability means that a person can give the disk to a colleague to work on. Flexibility means that users of optical disks can share information over different computing platforms. Removable optical disks will be interchangeable among different operating systems, under standards developed by the International Standards Organization. Sony's rewritable disks, for example, can be shared easily among an Apple Macintosh, an IBM PC/AT, a Sun workstation and a Compaq 386.

Optical disks now on the market store up to a few billion bytes, offer random access and are removable. This means that approximately fifty 12-

inch disks in a jukebox connected to a desktop computer and retrieve in seconds any piece of information from a database as large as 130 complete Encyclopedia Britannica.

The first optical disks, read-only videodiscs and audio CDs, have been available since the beginning of the decade. WORM disks have been available for almost as long. In the late 1980s, Sony Corporation became the first vendor to ship rewritable optical disk drives in volume.

Each of these three kinds of optical disks — read-only, write-once, and rewritable — is removable, has large storage capacities, and serves as a rotating computer memory. In addition, each has its own special characteristics and benefits.

Benefits of CD-ROM

The preeminent version of the read-only disc is the CD-ROM, which stands for Compact Disc Read-Only Memory. Sony, along with Philips N.V. of the Netherlands, invented the CD-ROM and developed its standards.

Physically, the CD-ROM disc is identical in size to the digital audio CD purchased in a record store. Because it is mass produced by injection molding, CD-ROM discs are extremely inexpensive to make. In 1990, the cost of a single replicated CD-ROM disc is under two dollars.

Since it is small, inexpensive, and can store large amounts of digital information, the CD-ROM is an ideal medium for distributing static information. The cost of distribution is in direct proportion to the value of the information, without being distorted by the price of the medium, exactly the same as with paper but unlike online information services, which must charge for time and connection in order to amortize large equipment costs.

CD-ROM discs are physically identical to audio CDs. They are the same size, use the same materials and the same manufacturing process and are close-to-the-same drive design. Their development has been almost entirely paid for by the extraordinary commercial success of audio CDs, which were introduced in 1982 and have already overtaken vinyl LPs in total unit sales. As a result, CD-ROM is far less expensive than any other medium, including paper, for distributing very large amounts of digital data.

The CD-ROM's genesis in the audio CD even determined its capacity, which is directly related to the playing time of an audio CD: seventy-four minutes and forty-four seconds (when produced under the best possible manufacturing conditions). That duration is neither accidental nor arbitrary. It is just sufficient to record the entire length of a certain version of Beethoven's Ninth Symphony especially beloved by the Sony Chairman Akio Morita — or so the story goes.

Benefits of Write-Once

CD-ROM is an inexpensive, standardized, electronic publishing media. It is not possible, however, to store new information on them once the master disks have been written. Writable optical disks come in two forms. The first is write-once disks, on which data, once written, are permanent. Write-once disks preserve a record of all transactions recorded on the WORM disk. This makes them the perfect medium for sensitive operations where it is important to keep an audit trail. All the successive versions of an engineering drawing, a contract or a ledger page, from day to day and week to week, are permanently preserved for inspection. In addition, the permanence of write-once disks has legal consequences. Since information cannot be altered on a write-once disk, it is more likely to be admissable as legal evidence than rewritable media.

Finally, write-once optical media is inexpensive. At eleven-cents per megabyte for 12-inch WORM disk, it is competitive with microfilm, paper, and magnetic tape — and far less expensive than magnetic disks. Since write-once is such an inexpensive storage medium, it is well suited for archiving information which cannot be altered and must be stored for a long period of time.

Benefits of Rewritable

Rewritable optical disks take the write-once concept and add the ability to erase and write over a spot on the disk. Therefore, they are more comparable to magnetic disks than are read-only or write-once optical disks because stored information can be changed multiple times.

Rewritable optical media is removable like a floppy diskette, but instead of holding about one megabyte like a floppy, or even 30-40MBs like a typical microcomputer Winchester hard disk, one double-sided rewritable optical disk holds 325MBs per side (depending upon sector size). A single 5.25-inch rewritable optical disk holds the equivalent of over twenty 32MB hard disks.

There are many untapped uses for the rewritable optical media. When the first 5MB hard disk drives came on the market a decade ago, few people could imagine filling up that more storage space with the personal computers then in use. However, ten years ago PCs were limited partly because mass storage was unavailable. As soon as such extensive storage became available, software programs began to take advantage of these capacities. The PC user soon had access to software applications formerly available only on minicomputers and mainframes: database management systems, spreadsheets, graphics programs and other software that produced large files. A decade ago, a quarter of a megabyte was a very large file on a PC.

Today, there are plenty of specialized applications — especially those generating graphic output — that produce very large data and image files. In addition, as PC users gain proficiency in creating files, there is an increasing tendency to retain them. Users are very reluctant to delete information including files they will surely never use again. Rewritable optical disks, with their enormous capacities, will foster the development of new applications that can generate even larger files, such as video applications already on the horizon. That is the nature of the computer revolution.

Rewritable Applications

One of the most important computer trends is using Local Area Networks (LANs) to connect various computers and peripherals within an organization. LANs represent the achievement of several ideas:

- An increased sharing of electronic information among co-workers
- A breaking down of the barriers of incompatibility between different kinds and sizes of computers
- The emergence of a completely new work environment in which, according to a computer industry CEO, the user will be able to access data without knowing, and more importantly, without caring where that data are stored.

The PC will not act as simply an extension of the mini- or mainframe computer. The minicomputer or mainframe will be an extension of the PC.

LANs will increasingly substitute for mainframes. This has extraordinary implications for the use of rewritable optical storage. For example, a LAN connecting twenty PCs using Intel 80386 microprocessors provides more processing power (as measured in MIPs) than most existing mainframes.

MIPs aside, LANs do not yet offer throughput to match mainframe channel speeds, but eventually they will because of fiber optic connections. When that day comes, LANs may well offer processing power, data transfer rates and, as a result of retrievable optical storage, mass storage capacity rivalling mainframe computers at a fraction of the cost. An added benefit would be flexibility: when a mainframe goes down, the whole system goes down. When a LAN workstation goes down, the other workstations keep on running.

Besides bringing the storage capacity of mainframes to a LAN, rewritable optical disks will bring interchangeability. Because a worldwide standard is being developed by the International Standards Organization (ISO) for rewritable optical disks, the convenience of rewritable optical storage will eventually extend to platform interchangeability. All rewritable optical disks will eventually be interchangeable among different operating system. Software developed by vendors will provide disk interchangeability even without further improvements in the ISO standard. This software will translate the file structures of various operating systems making it uncomplicated to read and write data on the same disk with, for example, a PC, Sun workstation, DEC MicroVAX and an Apple Macintosh. As optical storage's capacity can help turn LANs into substitutes for mainframes, their interchangeability will help transfer information among different LANs.

Connecting individuals within networks and connecting networks within larger networks multiplies the potential sharing of information. Subsequently shared information creates more information. When two pieces of information are combined, the result is often new information or even knowledge.

The advantages of security, interchangeability and flexibility will be available at individual workstations and in a single central repository. Rewritable optical disks will be used to hold all the data used on a network in a single central repository where removability will eliminate the headaches of backing up data. The file server will contain two disk drives. All data will be mirrored, that is written identically to both of them. At the end of the day, one rewritable optical disk can be taken out for back-up storage and other left in for the next day's work and changes.

Finally, LANs and Wide Area Networks (WANs) will become more efficient. Moreover, the global telephone network (ISDN) will become a digital network into which all other networks will connect. Interconnection and integration of computers with other digital devices, such as video displays, telephones and facsimile machines will occur at the same time as network interfaces become standardized, fiber optic cable increases the amount of transmissible information, and more powerful processors enhance and localize control of network functions.

Our ability to share information will grow enormously, but it will also demand some way for each of us to store our personal information; that way will be rewritable optical storage. In fact, without rewritable optical disks, the full potential of the coming network age might not be achievable.

Rewritable optical storage will also permit new applications where sharing information is less important but the ability to alter data, especially images, is required. Some of these possibilities already exist.

An example is a landscape architect designing the grounds of a new house in the mid-1990s. Data on the terrain have already been gathered and stored on large WORM disks with subsets distributed on CD-ROM for use by government planning agencies, utilities that install the water and sewer pipes, gas lines, electricity and fiber-optic multiple-data telecommunications cabling, and the contractor who grades the property. The landscaper buys a subset of that data on a small format rewritable disk for a PC. Using simulation software and a gardening database on a CD-ROM disc, a view of the future of the grounds is instantly simulated. A maple tree is planted at one location and an image of what it will look like and where its shadow will fall in five years is created. The landscaper sees that it will shadow the vegetable garden so he moves it to another corner of the grounds. The landscape continues to select plants to fit the terrain and climate and to move them around on screen until satisfied. Each time a move is made, a portion of the evolving plan is rewritten making good use of the rewritable capability of the optical drive. When done, seeds, bulbs and saplings are automatically ordered from a list generated by PC and stored on the rewritable optical disk based on pricing contained in the original CD-ROM gardening database which also contained advertising for various nurseries that offer order-by-modem services.

Today there are image simulation applications in use requiring optical storage's capacity. For example, a weight loss clinic can take a patient's photo, use a scanner to digitize it and store it as a computer file. It then uses image editing software to remove excess pounds, add make-up, change hairstyles, and perhaps dress the client in a new wardrobe. The result is before-and-after photos at the beginning of the therapy instead of at the end. Obviously, this can be a powerful motivator for the client's health.

Such imaging systems require and use a considerable amount of mass storage. Since most images need to be altered, rewritable optical is the perfect medium. The use of rewritable optical disk in plastic surgery is obvious. Applications are also being used by law enforcement agencies to automate the creation of artists' sketches of suspects. Advertising agencies are using rewritable optical disk to test-market designs for advertisements and labels. Film and video production companies are using rewritable optical storage to create storyboards and to evaluate designs for sets, costumes, lighting, and other elements of production.

Image synthesis and design applications will have other uses. Business presentations will easily be customized to each audience. An architect will try out different versions of a building on a screen. A mechanical engineer will play with the design of a product, its subassemblies and the parts of each sub-assembly, until the balance required by manufacturing constraints is achieved.

There are other applications for rewritable optical disks that have nothing to do with images. Since hotels keep records of their customers, a database of all the customers who stay in a large hotel over the course of ten years, for example, is too big to manage economically on magnetic disks. Rewritable optical disks can be used in such systems and connected with the hotel's reservation management system. In some cases retrieval of the guest's record will be automatic (in response to the guest's home or office phone number) and will be delivered to the called party as a feature of its telephone service. This kind of service is already available in selected locations and will be used nationwide by the early 1990s.

Such precision helps the hotel to remain competitive. The same holds true for hospitals, both for cost-cutting and physician referrals. Consider the possibilities of applying the same techniques to telemarketing, shopping by phone, or any other aspect of customer relations.

Rewritable optical storage is already inexpensive, and getting more so. Comparison between optical rewritable and magnetic rewritable hard disks is tricky because magnetic disks are not removable (the exception is the Bernoulli Box). For most PC users, to obtain the magnetic hard disk, a drive must be purchased. Since optical disks are removable, users need to purchase only one drive to use any number of disks. The comparison on a dollar-per-MB basis for non-removable rewritable magnetic hard disk and rewritable optical disks is dramatic: a 650MB rewritable optical disk costs about $350 or 54 cents per MB. A rewritable magnetic disk and drive with a comparable capacity would cost about $4,500, or $6.92 per MB.

The price of rewritable optical technology can be expected to fall rapidly. Less than ten years ago the first VCR cost $1,500. Today, comparable models cost a tenth of that. Semiconductor memory prices drop by half every two years. Rewritable optical will have a similar cost curve, and eventually become so inexpensive that it will be a standard peripheral similar to today's floppy drive. In a few years, we will be using laptop computers with built-in rewritable optical drives and three-inch disks carrying in our pockets as much data as the National Archives now stores in several rooms.

Combined Applications

Perhaps the most intriguing optical storage applications involve combinations. In a few years, mass market microcomputers may have only two forms of storage both of which will be optical: a rewritable drive and a CD-ROM or similar read-only drive. This combination will be adequate for all the needs of a general purpose business workstation. In such a workstation, mass storage performs three functions: data distribution, working storage, and backup. Data distribution will be shared by CD-ROM and rewritable optical disks. The CD-ROM drive will deliver reference databases and very large software/documentation packages. Rewritable optical drives will deliver small software packages as well as working storage and backup.

Farther down the road, all these functions will be combined into a single, small-format multifunction optical drive capable of using both rewritable and read-only optical media. For example, within a few years, we might see a drive that can read, write and erase M-O disks that are about 3.5-inch in diameter and can read small CD-ROM discs of the same size. Sony and Philips NV have jointly proposed a 200MB CD-ROM disc measuring 80mm (about 3.2 inches) in diameter.

A multifunction, or hybrid, drive using both rewritable and read-only disks opens the prospect of future computers using nothing but optical disks as their only form of mass storage. Such a drive, in the 80 to 90mm size range, would be faster since the optical head would have less disk geography to cover and because the lighter disks could be spun much faster. Also, technical advances will eliminate the need to erase and rewrite data on an M-O disk on separate revolutions. The performance of such multifunction drives will match or exceed that of magnetic disks. Multifunctional optical disk drives will have greater capacities and cost only slightly more than today's rewritable optical disk drives. We may well see a single optical disk containing one section of read-only data as well as another blank section that is rewritable. Such a hybrid M-O/ROM disk would be made of polycarbonate plastic as both CD-ROM and M-O disks are today.

A hybrid optical disk would be the ideal medium for distributing large databases meant to be used differently by each user. Imagine a single hybrid optical disk containing a read-only version of a whole bookshelf of reference material and a rewritable workspace on which a person could add personal annotations, pathways and additional data files. No magnetic disk could ever provide this kind of flexibility because data distributed on magnetic disks must be written electronically. Even on high-speed copying machines it is impossible to write data to magnetic disks at anywhere near the speeds with which hybrid M-O/read-only memory disks could be stamped out.

Offering unique advantages, a hybrid optical disk would not compete with magnetic disks on performance. Such a disk, used for data distribution, would have to adhere to a recognized standard for compatibility and interchangeability. ISO has developed such a standard for rewritable M-O disks; both Sony and 3M support this standard fir M-O disks. In the future a similar international standard will no doubt be developed for hybrid optical disks as well.

Beside disks, the principles of optical storage can be applied to strips of flexible media. In lengths of hundreds of feet long, these will be used on reels as optical tape. In lengths of two or three inches, they will be affixed to pieces of plastic like credit cards. Optical tape will be used to capture the literally astronomical amounts of data sent back from satellites. One of the first of such installations of optical tape using the CREO Optical Tape Recorder was at the Canadian Center for Remote Sensing in mid-1989. Optical tape may also be used to record high-definition television (HDTV), and for a myriad of other uses demanding enormous mass storage capacity without random retrieval. At the other end of the spectrum, a single optical memory card carried in one's wallet, purse or pocket, will store about 700 typed pages or about thirty newspaper-quality photographs, or a combination of the two.

Optical tape is barely on the verge of commercial use, and optical cards may be somewhat farther away. However, optical disks are most emphatically impacting the market today.

Conclusion

Optical storage, like any other technology, is most significant in the ways it enhances, complements and supports related information technologies. Technology is not important for its' own sake, but is a means of satisfying human needs and accomplishing human goals.

Optical storage supports an historical trend of the past few decades: the trend toward digitizing information, to make it easier to automate its transmission and processing, thereby making it available to a growing number of groups of individuals and organizations. The full power of computers can be applied only to digital information, and for many years the world's information has been undergoing a quiet transformation from the analog to the digital state. In the future, virtually all information will originate in a digital form, whether it is video, audio, x-rays, satellite information, or graphics. All information will be accessible to computers — that is, to any personal workstation with sufficient mass storage.

It will be accessible in its original condition, since information will be created in digital form. Slides created at a personal workstation using desktop presentation software will look exactly the same to their audience as they did at the moment of their creation. A page of text, typeset in any combination of fonts, containing any sort of graphic special effects, will look exactly the same on the printed page as on the screen where it was created. Until now, automated communication exists only by paying a penalty in design constraints.

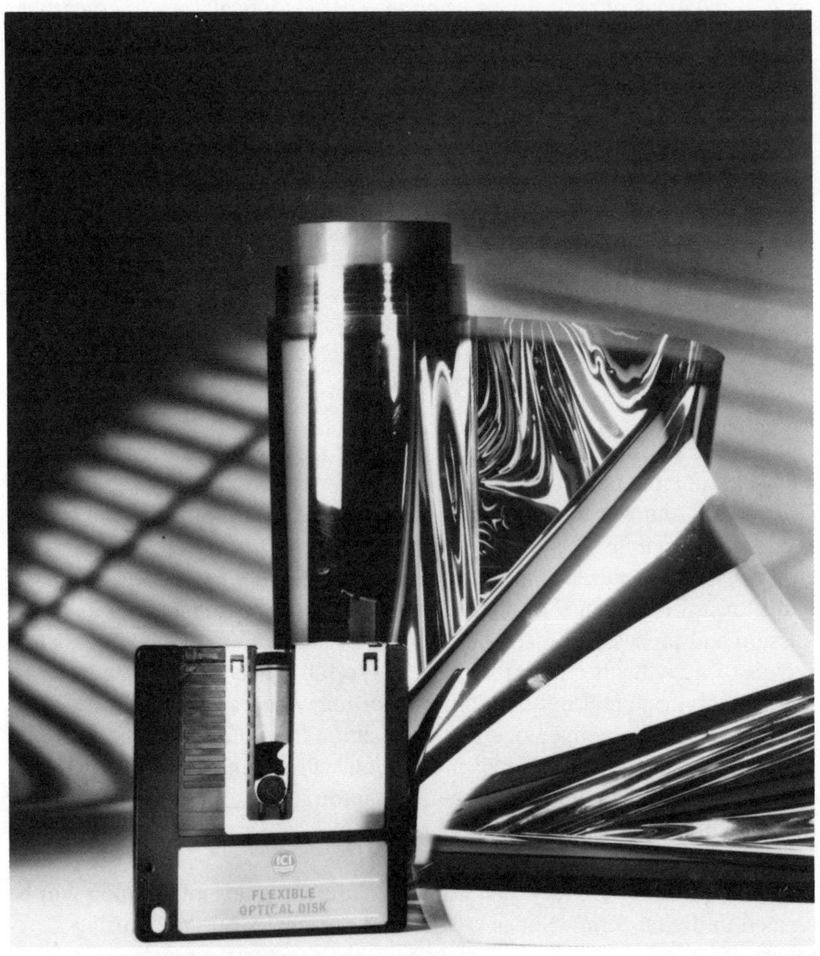

ICI Imagedata has developed Digital Paper^{tm}, a flexible write-once optical tape medium which can be inserted into cassettes, cut into strips or tags, and disk cartridges. (Courtesy, ICI Imagedata)

These new capabilities will vastly enhance the effectiveness of our electronic communications. They cannot happen without mass storage. For example, a powerful desktop publishing system based on digital typography and graphics requires all three kinds of mass storage: read-only, rewritable, and write-once. CD-ROM discs will be used as online databases, holding enormous files containing limitless digital typefaces and fonts, catalogs of clip art and reference materials such as dictionaries, thesauri, books of quotations, and design handbooks. Rewritable optical disks will be used to store works-in-progress, from single pages to large volumes, including multiple versions pending choice of a final design. Finally, when the work is in its final form, it will be written to a WORM optical disk for storage and reference. In addition, these WORM disks will be used to build in-house libraries of customized alterations of materials distributed originally on CD-ROM.

Since there is so much information in the world and it is difficult to correlate, the only way to use information meaningfully, is to specialize. Specialization, however, has its penalties. It tends to reduce communication between people working in different disciplines. At a time when solutions to global problems seem to demand cross-disciplinary cooperation and the sharing of ideas, it is vital to balance specialization with enhanced communication, to make more information accessible to more people in more ways. Towards this end, optical storage will justify the billions of dollars that have been invested in it.

3
Software Considerations for Rewritable and Multifunction Optical Drives

Brian A. Berg

Although the software development effort required for rewritable optical disk drives is less complex than that of write-once (WORM) drives, the characteristics of currently available rewritable optical disk technology invoke special considerations with which an integrator must be concerned. Optical storage standards, magneto-optical (M-O) media, and the recent availability of phase-change media and multifunction optical disk drives also present software integration and performance issues that must be understood in order to create an efficient and adaptable product.

Software for WORM vs. Rewritable Media

To appreciate the software integration complexities of WORM optical devices, it is best to compare these drives with their rewritable optical counterparts. There is no better way to achieve this than looking at the rate which these two optical disk drive types have penetrated the market.

Although WORM drives became available in 1984 and 1985, sales of this high-capacity random access device have always lagged projections. Even though WORM's non-volatility had a definite appeal to some market segments, support software was slow to emerge. Rewritable optical disk drives finally became available in mid-1988 following years of expectation and vaporware. Unlike WORM, rewritable drive integrators have been quick to release software packages for major computer platforms.

The primary reason for the faster acceptance of rewritable drives as compared with write-once is clear: *The write-once nature of WORM media creates a difficult software integration task in a world where most popular operating systems assume the use of a directly rewritable media for the storage of data files.*

While WORM technology has satisfied the needs of many users who required a high-capacity and removable random access media, its write-once characteristic has been a burden to some users. Although many predict its demise, WORM technology has found a market niche with users who require archivability and data security. Many users who are not concerned about nonvolatility, but still require a high-capacity, removable media are now using rewritable devices.

Comparing Rewritable Optical Storage Technologies

Since rewritable optical media is indeed just that — rewritable — its integration is a far simpler chore since it can generally be used just like the well entrenched magnetic drives. All rewritable drives on the market used magneto-optical (M-O) technology until Panasonic announced its phase-change (P-C) multifunction optical disk drive in mid-1990. A third technique using organic dye-polymer (D-P) media was originally thought to have promise for rewritable devices, but it now appears destined only for write-once usage (WORM drives from Pioneer and Ricoh use D-P media). While the Canon M-O, Panasonic P-C and Ricoh D-P drives do not use ANSI/ISO standard media, virtually all other rewritable drives do.

M-O has the unique but unfortunate requirement that sectors must be erased before they are written, and currently all drives perform this erasure on a separate pass over the media. However, since P-C devices are directly rewritable (they permit new data to be written over old data in a single pass), they would appear to have a performance advantage.

Unlike M-O, P-C media is written by changing the molecular structure of the optical disk. This fact limits the number of rewrite cycles that the media can endure. Thus, prudency dictates that data be verified after it is written. Because verification involves a separate pass over the media, P-C and M-O both require two media passes for data to be written in an assured manner.

Although P-C's requirement for a verify pass over the media may be questioned by some, WORM drives have typically performed this verify function by default. Typically, M-O optical disk drives do not perform a verify pass since media is verified at format time and writing does not involve a structural change of the disk material.

In anticipation of P-C media sectors failing, the Panasonic multifunction optical disk drive allows the user to declare an area of the disk to have the number of times its sectors are written monitored. Any such sector that is written 300,000 times is automatically remapped to a "spare" area. If it is written another 300,000 writes, it is remapped again. However, if this happens again (after a total of 900,000 writes to the logical sector), an error will result. As most file systems require a disk's lowest numbered sectors to be rewritten the most often, this area is typically the one that would need to be monitored by the drive's firmware.

Mitigating Poor Performance

Since a two-pass write operation is a fact of life for current rewritable optical disk technology, the software integrator should attempt to minimize its impact. As the P-C verify pass must be performed before the write operation can be considered complete, there appears to be no way to improve P-C write performance. An M-O write operation, however, would require only one pass when a sector is requested to be written. This will be true if the following assumptions are made:

- A newly formatted disk is always totally erased.
- The drive's firmware has an ERASE command and its WRITE command has an Erase By-Pass (EBP) option.
- Disk sectors are erased during the time between when they are de-allocated from one file and re-allocated to another file.

If the first assumption is not already addressed by the drive's internal format command, a utility could be easily written to erase disks before they are considered available for use. The second assumption is addressed by the new SCSI-2 standard, and virtually all rewritable optical drives are available with a SCSI interface.

The third assumption requires that a list of sectors to be erased and a list of sectors already erased are maintained by the operating system or a system utility, and that these lists are written to a special area on each disk. When sectors are erased, sector numbers are moved from the to-be-erased list to the already-erased list. Under multitasking operating systems such as UNIX, OS/2, and DEC-VMS, sector erasure could be performed periodically by a "background" utility as well as when a disk is dismounted. A TSR (Terminate and Stay Resident) program can perform this chore under MS-DOS, although a special utility to mount and dismount media would also be needed to insure the two lists are flushed to disk before the media can be removed.

Companies that are reportedly considering this level of operating system support under their own versions of UNIX include NeXT, Inc. under Mach, and Hewlett-Packard Co. (HP) under HP-UX. HP believes that the mitigation of the erase pass is crucial to the development of a high-performance rewritable optical file management system.

A Universal Logical Format for Rewritable Media

X3B11.1, the ANSI accredited committee for Optical Disk Volume and File Structure Standards, is working to create a logical file interchange standard for optical media, i.e., an optical file system (see *Optical Information Systems*, Vol. 10 No. 2, pp. 84-89). Their immediate target is WORM media, but their work should be immediately extensible to rewritable media as well. Although virtually all rewritable implementations today support the native file system of the host computer, the removable optical media that they use cannot be read or written under other operating systems without special software to interpret the "foreign" file system.

Were a disk format encompassing the requirements of all major file system formats to exist, such translation software would likely become widely available. The result of such a phenomenon would be a nearly universally usable, high-capacity, random access media. The potential ramifications of such a format are great indeed.

HP is developing a product based on the X3B11.1 standard which will incorporate the M-O performance enhancement described earlier, and has proposed use of this enhancement to the X3B11.1 committee.

Media Sector Size Issues

The ANSI/ISO standard for the physical characteristics of rewritable 5.25-inch optical media includes two variants of sector size: 512 and 1024 user bytes per sector. (Media sector size is determined at the time it is manufactured.) If both media types are to be accommodated, the possibility of two sector sizes presents a software integration issue for the following reasons:

- At most only one of these sizes will match the sector size of an operating system's native file system.

- Media of a sector size other than that of the native file system may not be bootable.

The first issue is solved by proper buffering of data, but a performance problem exists for write operations if the file system sector size is smaller than that of the media being used. Writing a 512-byte sector to 1024-byte media requires that a 1024-byte sector be read, that it be merged with the 512 bytes to be written, and that the sector be erased (if magneto-optical), the new sector data written and the sector verified (if phase-change). This write operation requires three passes over the media for both M-O and P-C media.

The second issue is of concern if a system's boot ROM code is tied to a fixed sector size for the boot device. Since 512 bytes is the base sector size for operating systems such as UNIX, MS-DOS, OS/2, DEC-VMS, and Apple Macintosh, the bootability of 1024-byte media on these systems is a potential problem. Some vendors have overcome this in SCSI host adapter firmware for MS-DOS and device driver software for the Macintosh by implementing a data merging algorithm for write operations (as just described) and a data extraction algorithm for reading, but it poses a problem for operating systems such as SunOS (Sun Microsystems' version of UNIX).

Removable Media Issues

The removability feature of optical media has been mentioned in a positive context herein, but it does pose a software development and integration challenge for the following reasons:

- A disk's file system must be in a quiescent state before the disk can be allowed to be removed.
- It must be possible to distinguish any one platter from all others.
- Media swapping such as that required by a multi-platter volume should be allowed.

The first point is only an issue if the host operating system buffers write data and may declare an operation complete before the media is actually written, as is the case with UNIX and other multitasking operating systems. This issue can probably be addressed through use of the SCSI PREVENT/ALLOW MEDIUM REMOVAL command to insure that a piece of media can be considered fixed while its file system is dynamic.

The second point is of particular concern for installations that have data stored on a large set of disks that often need to be swapped in and out of drives within an optical jukebox. Each disk surface must contain some unique identification (ID) in a label field in order for it to be correctly identified.

Since most operating systems do not allow for such a field (or at least one that can virtually guarantee uniqueness), a special file or area on the disk must be set aside to retain this ID. The ID should be created and written only when the disk is first used, and could be constructed from the date, time, a serial number, a system drive number, and a random number.

The third point requires that a requested platter, such as one that is part of a multi-volume set, be made available when necessary. This requirement can be smoothly accomodated if media swapping is automated, for example, a jukebox is available for this chore. Manual swapping, however, requires that an operator be requested to insert a particular platter (whose identity can be verified by its unique ID field). Operating systems such as UNIX have no standard way to allow for such operator interaction because most flavors of UNIX have no concept of a removable medium.

Accommodating High-Capacity Media

The large data space on the surface of a rewritable optical disk (128MB to 500MB) has posed a problem for some operating systems that expected media to never surpass, for example, 32MB in size (as was the case for earlier versions of MS-DOS). Today, the lastest versions of most popular software platforms have no problem in this regard. As a result, integrators should be aware of the minimum requirements for the environment in which their software can operate.

The SCSI Interface

As previously mentioned, virtually all rewritable optical drives are available with a SCSI interface. SCSI is popular for a number of reasons, including the fact that SCSI has been a standard feature on Apple Macintosh and Sun Microsystems' computers since around 1985. SCSI-based devices tend to be "plug-and-play" on such platforms, further encouraging SCSI's proliferation.

The SCSI INQUIRY command is used by a host to detemine information about a device including its type, vendor ID, and revision level. Although the standard SCSI device type designation for rewritable optical drives is "optical memory device", most vendors have chosen to use "direct-access device". Since the latter is what is expected to be used by a magnetic disk, use of rewritable drives as if they were magnetic is more easily facilitated. It should be noted, though, that accommodating any special rewritable media requirements (such as the technique described earlier in the "Mitigating Poor Performance" section) requires special handling by a device driver.

The SCSI-2 CAM Committee

SCSI provides a generic set of commands for use by a wide variety of device types. Due to this, the integrator's job is simplified since special device considerations (such as defect management) are handled in the device itself. A device driver, however, is required for platforms lacking a standard SCSI port. Since there has been no standard protocol for setting up and issuing SCSI commands on such platforms, the SCSI standards committee organized an *ad hoc* group known as the SCSI-2 Common Access Method (CAM) Committee.

Although the CAM Committee has had some problems finalizing such a protocol, in mid-1990 Microsoft, Western Digital, Compaq, Adaptec, and NCR announced a layered device-driver architecture called LADDR which defines a protocol for OS/2. In addition, IBM finally endorsed SCSI with its introduction of two Micro Channel Architecture host adapters in April, 1990.

The CAM Committee is now focused on defining a protocol for UNIX and Novell Netware.

Integrating Multifunction Optical Disk Drives

After much anticipation, multifunction optical disk drives that can read and write both write-once and rewritable media were first shown or announced by some vendors including Pioneer and Panasonic in mid-1990. The following four technology approaches are being used:

- Write-once ablative and rewritable magneto-optical
- Write-once dye-polymer and rewritable magneto-optical
- Write-once and rewritable, both using phase-change
- Write-once and rewritable, both using magneto-optical

Unlike the last two approaches, the first two require circuitry to handle two disparate technologies, increasing drive cost and the manufacturer's engineering effort. The Panasonic P-C media for the third approach is identical for WORM and rewritable except for a difference in the optical sensing material and in media designators indicating in WORM versus rewritable. HP, which announced support for the last approach along with thirteen other drive, media, and computer vendors, uses identical M-O media except for a code molded into the media indicating WORM versus rewritable.

Multifunction optical disk drives for all approaches have firmware that handles the media correctly, including disallowing sector overwrites on write-once media. Since the last approach uses M-O media even for write-once usage, the media is erased as the last step of the drive's SCSI FORMAT command.

Integrating a multifunction drive requires software to detect the current media type and insure that all driver and applications software treat the media as write-once or rewritable. Hence, media type must be checked when the drive is first accessed and whenever there is a media change. Although the current media type can be determined from the Peripheral Device Type byte returned by the SCSI INQUIRY command, there is an important caveat regarding rewritable media in "The SCSI Interface" section of this chapter. Even though the drive itself will not allow sectors on write-once media to be overwritten, applications software that uses different algorithms based on the media type must be aware of the current media loaded. The integrator also must be aware of other ramifications of having to swap between media types while an application is up and running.

Interestingly, although the Pioneer/LMSI/Optimem drive (which uses the second approach — magneto-optical) can sense the type of media loaded, it requires the device driver to determine the current type of media with the SCSI READ MODE command, and possibly allow for its use with the SCSI CHANGE MODE command. Both of these are vendor unique commands which switch the drive circuitry between write-once and rewritable, including turning the M-O magnetic coil "on" or "off" as appropriate.

Conclusion

Rewritable optical disk drives are generally easy to integrate into today's computer systems since their logical operation is identical to that of today's widely available magnetic disk drives. Issues, however, regarding poor write performance, dual sector sizes, removability, and the availability of multifunction drives must be addressed by system integrators interested in creating versatile systems with good performance.

Its rewritability, removability, and high-capacity have made rewritable optical media the best candidate for an interchangable medium among disparate operating systems. When the ANSI X3B11.1 committee standardizes a generic file system for write-once and rewritable optical disk media, the necessary elements will be in place for universal interchangeability.

4
Development of a Flexible Rewritable Optical Storage Medium

Geoffrey A. Russell

From its conception optical storage has been regarded as having several advantages over magnetic storage for large capacity applications. Principal advantages cited are:

- *High data density* is due to the large number of tracks per inch achievable with a laser beam focused to a spot size of 1μm or less. This leads to a tenfold increase in areal data density over magnetic media.

- *Data integrity* is increased due to freedom from head crash, improved EMI resistance, media removability, and materials stability.

- *Lower cost per megabyte* can be achieved due to the high data density of optical media. This reduces space and allows much-more data to be kept online and available to users.

To date, optical storage has not been able to displace magnetic storage, nor has it found other high-volume applications such as replacement of paper hardcopy. The chief barriers to large-scale acceptance of optical storage are:

- Inexperience with the operating characteristics of optical storage. Applications developers, system integrators and users are still learning how to take advantage of large volumes of online data.

- Optical system performance characteristics, particularly in the areas of access time and data transfer rates, limit optical storage in high-performance applications.

- High cost per megabyte due to the low volumes of media required for existing applications has limited optical storage to large systems.

While media costs will undoubtedly come down as the volume of media required increases, there are inherent limitations on the reductions which can be made in media price due to the expensive manufacturing processes involved in the production of any of the current types of optical media. Substrate molding, vacuum metallization, spin-coating and the other processes used have high capital equipment requirements, low throughput rates and poor materials utilization rates.

Web-Coating Offers Lower Media Cost

In order for the costs of optical media to be reduced sufficiently to compete with magnetic media in high-volume applications, a new type of manufacturing process will be required. The process most likely to reduce media cost is web-coating of optical media onto flexible substrates. This process has already been described for a write-once optical medium, and a joint venture has been established by ICI Chemicals (United Kingdom) and Iomega (Roy, Idaho) to develop an optical drive using Bernoulli stabilization to allow the use of optical media coated on a flexible polyester substrate (Pountain, 1989; Perera, 1989).

Optical Data, Inc. (ODI) has developed a rewritable optical media technology based upon the use of dyed polymer films which is also well-suited to production by web-coating methods. This chapter will describe the basic operating principles of the ODI medium, briefly discuss the web-coating process by which the medium can be produced, and summarize the results of preliminary experiments in the production of the ODI rewritable optical medium by web-coating. A summary of the product development schedule, probable product characteristics and media costs is also provided

Principles of ODI Rewritable Optical Medium

The structure and operating principles of ODI's rewritable optical storage medium have been described in detail elsewhere (Lind and Hartman, 1988; Halter and Iwamoto, 1988; Skiens and Russell, 1989). The structure of the

ODI medium is shown in Figure 1. For rigid media applications the substrate-incident structure shown on the right is preferred. For flexible media applications the simpler air-incident structure on the left is preferred. In both cases, the ODI medium has two dyed active layers, a soft elastomeric layer (the *expansion layer*) and a rigid glassy layer (the *retention layer*). The expansion layer contains a dye or pigment which absorbs at one wavelength, _W. The retention layer contains a dye which absorbs at a second wavelength, _E. The current write wavelength is 840nm, and the current erase wavelength is 780nm. These correspond to the two commonest laser diode emission lines currently available. The processes by which data is written, read and erased are shown in Figure 2.

Write Process

Data is written onto the ODI medium using a high-powered 840nm laser pulse, typically 5 to 10mW at the media surface. Absorption of the laser photons by the expansion layer dye causes the expansion layer to heat up rapidly. The resulting thermal expansion creates a vertical stress. The warming of the

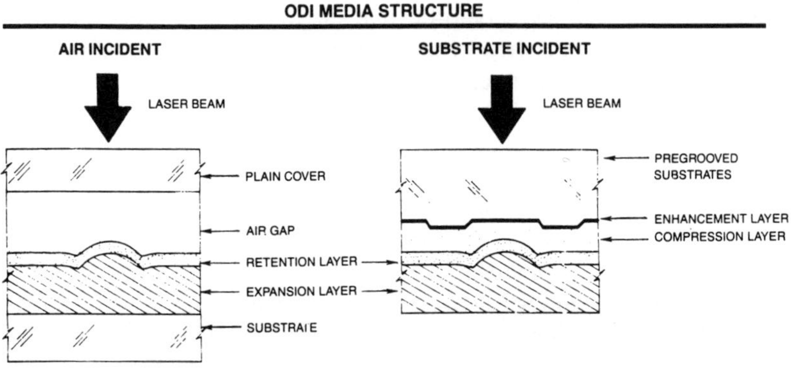

Figure 1. Air Incident and Substrate Incident Media Configuration. (Courtesy, ODI)

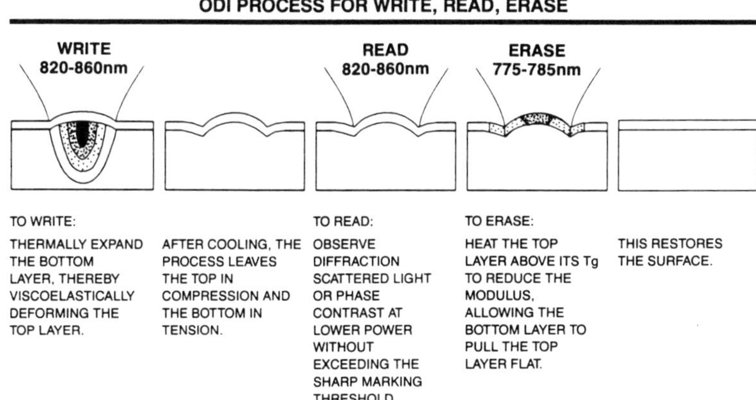

ODI PROCESS FOR WRITE, READ, ERASE
WRITE
820-860nm
READ
820-860nm
ERASE
775-785nm
TO WRITE:
THERMALLY EXPAND THE BOTTOM LAYER, THEREBY VISCOELASTICALLY DEFORMING THE TOP LAYER.
AFTER COOLING, THE PROCESS LEAVES THE TOP IN COMPRESSION AND THE BOTTOM IN TENSION.
TO READ:
OBSERVE DIFFRACTION SCATTERED LIGHT OR PHASE CONTRAST AT LOWER POWER WITHOUT EXCEEDING THE SHARP MARKING THRESHOLD.
TO ERASE:
HEAT THE TOP LAYER ABOVE ITS Tg TO REDUCE THE MODULUS, ALLOWING THE BOTTOM LAYER TO PULL THE TOP LAYER FLAT.
THIS RESTORES THE SURFACE.

Figure 2. ODI Process for Write, Read, Erase. (Courtesy, ODI).

retention layer by conduction softens it, allowing a mark to form on the top surface of the retention layer as the expansion layer swells. When the laser pulse ends, heat diffuses radially from the heated zone. The retention layer cools below its glass transition temperature (Tg) before the expansion layer can fully cool. This freezes in some of the strain caused by the thermal expansion leaving a mark. Typical mark dimensions are 0.8μm width, 0.8 to 3.0μm length (depending only on the length of the laser pulse) and 80 to 120nm in height.

Read Process

Data is read by tracking over the surface with a low-power laser beam, typically 0.5 to 1.5mW. Either 840nm or 780nm laser radiation can be used, although 840nm is generally preferred to avoid accidental erasure. Data signals are generated by scattering from the mark. As the beam from the objective

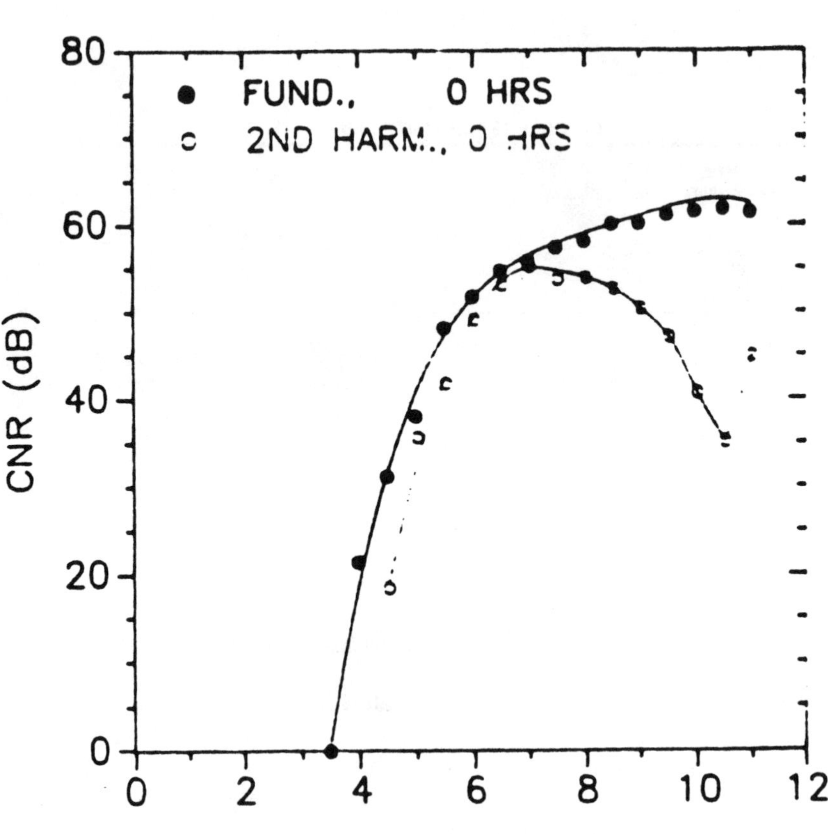

Figure 3. CNR vs Power for Al Media. Linear Velocity 3.00m/s; Write and Read Wavelength 840 nm; Duty Cycle - 50 percent. (Courtesy, ODI)

lens passes over the leading edge of the mark, the amount of energy returned from the media surface decreases due to scattering from the mark. When the beam passes over the trailing edge of the mark, scattering ceases, and the reflected energy returns to its baseline value.

Erase Process

Data is erased by irradiating the media with a 780nm laser pulse, which warms and softens the retention layer. The stress stored in the expansion

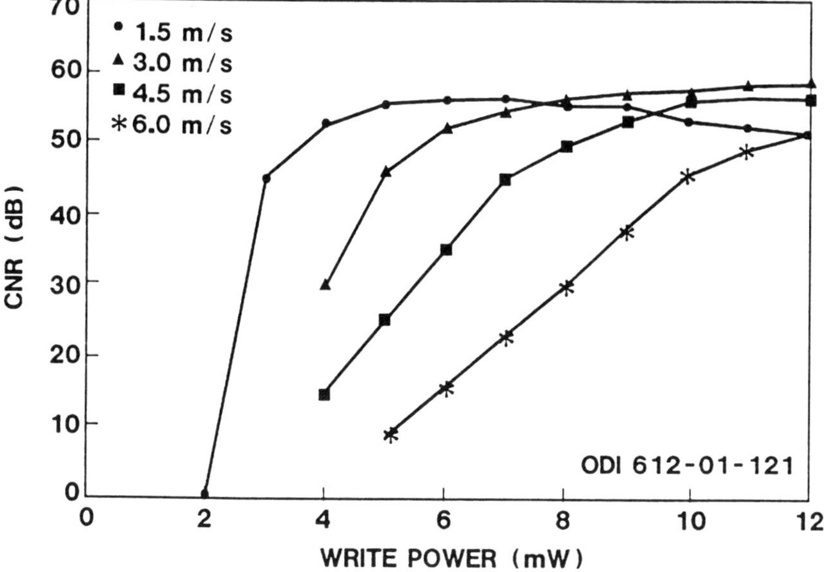

Figure 4. CNR vs write power and linear velocity. The media shows true energy density dependent marketing characteristics. Contrast and threshold are dependent only on the energy density of the writing beam and consequently scale precisely with the linear velocity of the media. The phenomena is best illustrated using the lower sensitivity media shown in the figure. (Courtesy, ODI)

layer when the retention layer cooled is used to pull the retention layer surface back to its original planar shape.

ODI Rewritable Medium Performance

CNR versus write power and linear velocity

Carrier-to-noise ratio (CNR) versus write pulse power is shown in Figure 3 for data written at 3.0m/s at 1 MHz with a 50 percent duty cycle. The medium exhibits a sharp marking threshold at 3.0mW, and achieves a CNR of 55 to 60dB at write powers in excess of 6.0mW. The effect of linear velocity on media performance is shown in Figure 4 for linear velocities ranging from 1.5 to 9.0m/s. As the linear velocity increases, the power required to achieve a CNR of 55dB increases proportionally. However, the ultimate CNR reached is independent of linear velocity, given sufficient laser power. This power/ time reciprocity allows the media to be used over a range of linear velocities from 1.2m/s, which is typical for CD applications to the 10m/s or greater which will be required to achieve dynamic stabilization in a Bernoulli drive.

Mark size and uniformity

Very high track densities can be achieved on the ODI medium. This is illustrated in Figure 5, which shows a series of tracks which have been written at track pitches which varied from 3.8μm down to 0.8μm. For reference, current CD-ROM discs and WORM disks use a track pitch of 1.6μm. On the ODI medium adjacent tracks are well-separated down to a spacing of 1.0μm. As the technology for preformatting improves to allow smaller track pitch and as the wavelengths of laser diodes decrease, the ODI medium will be capable of achieving higher densities, whereas other media technologies such as phase change and magneto-optic (M-O) will not due to their larger domain sizes.

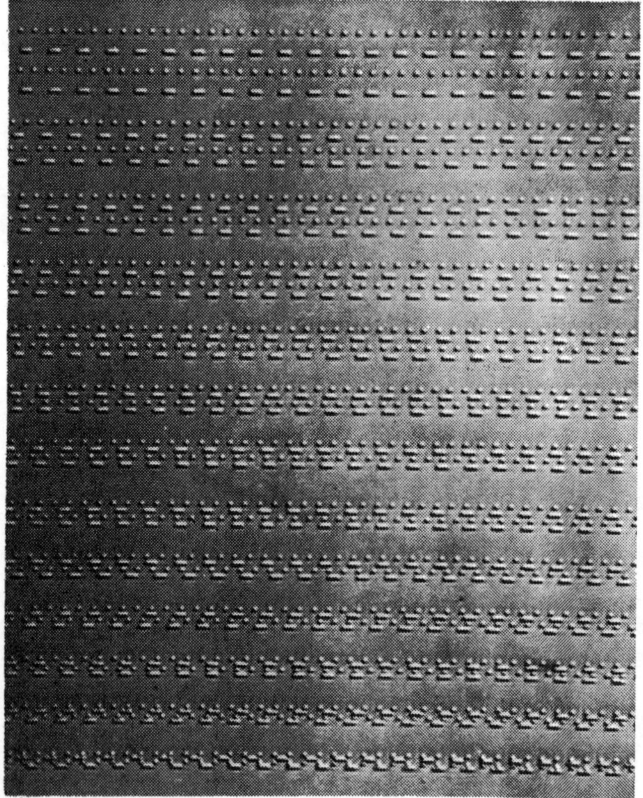

Figure 5. ODI Media - Track Separation, 3.8um to 0.8um. (Courtesy, ODI)

Mark formation on the ODI medium is very uniform and reproducible, as shown in the time interval analyzer trace which is shown in Figure 6. A series of marks was written on the disk using uncompensated write pulse lengths of 333ns, 400ns and 467ns, corresponding to mark lengths of 1.0μm, 1.2μm and 1.4μm. These mark lengths are typical of those used in EFM and other encoding schemes. All three mark lengths are well-separated in the time interval analysis, with no other data signals present. (The small peak at the right of the TIA trace is an artifact of the electronics.) This indicates that the ODI medium is capable of supporting EFM and other run-length encoding schemes to increase data density on the disk.

ODI MEDIA MARK LENGTH UNIFORMITY

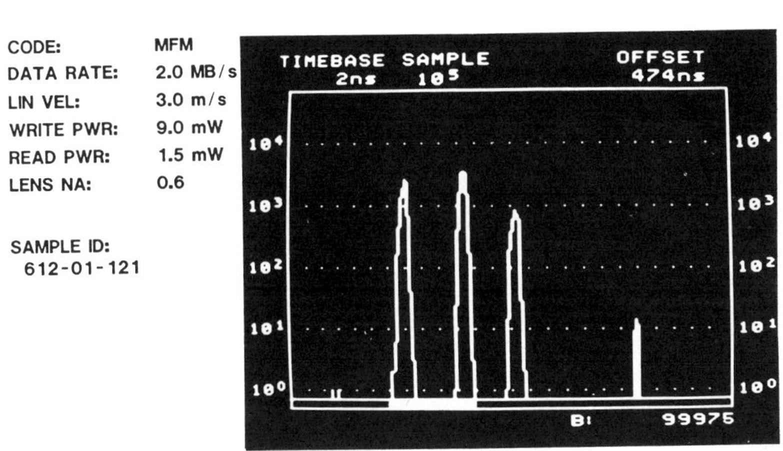

Figure 6. ODI Media Mark Length Uniformity (Courtesy, ODI). Mark separation for simple 2.0 Mb/s EFM is excellent as (3.0 m.s).

Erasure and cycling performance

Erasure performance is illustrated in Figure 7. The CNR versus write power curve for the sample was established as shown. Data was then written on the disk at a write power of 7mW which yielded a CNR after writing of 55dB. The data was then erased using a cw 780nm beam of varying intensity. The CNR after erasure was determined as a function of the erase power, as shown

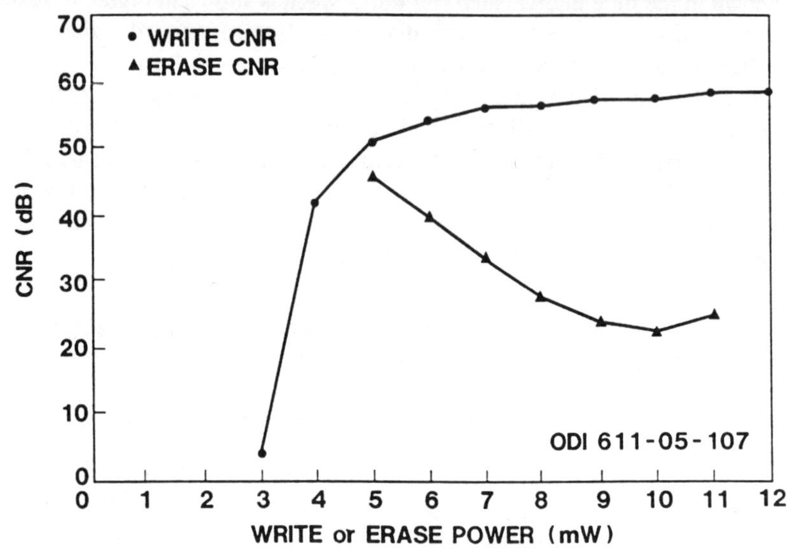

Figure 7. CNR vs Power for Both Write and Erase After Write. (Courtesy, ODI)

in the figure. At 5mW, a suppression of only 10dB was observed in the CNR. However, as the erase power was increased to 10mW, signal suppression improved until it exceeded 30dB suppression at 10mW erase power. This is ample suppression to allow the drive to reuse the erased sector for new data.

Performance of the medium as a function of write/erase cycling is shown in Figure 8. Here we show the spectrum analyzer traces after the first write and the corresponding erasure and compare them to the traces after the one thousandth write and its corresponding erasure. The write signal is well-suppressed in both cases, and there has been no increase in the noise floor during cycling, indicating that there has been no ablation or debris formation on the surface of the medium. Cycle lifetime of the medium is not infinite, however. Once the number of write/erase cycles exceeds 2000 to 5000, there is a rapid decrease in the CNR for newly-written data, and an increase in the CNR after erasure. This limits the use of the medium in certain applications. However, as the relationships between materials properties and media performance are better-defined, media cyclability is expected to improve substantially.

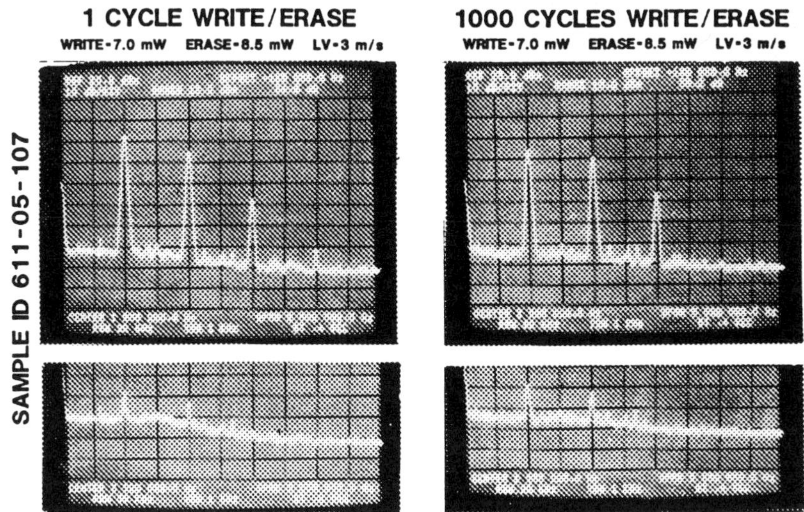

Figure 8. ODI Media Write/Erase Signal Spectrum. (Courtesy, ODI) Shown are typical write and erase CNR signals after 1 and 1000 cycles. There is little difference for a small drop in write CNR which occurs after the first cycle.

Environmental stability

One advantage of dye-in-polymer media as well as the ODI medium is their inherent oxidative stability. Unlike thin metal films, which must be protected against oxidation, phase separation and grain boundary growth, amorphous polymer films are thermally and oxidatively stable. As a result, media structures are simplified because passivation layers and oxygen-impermeable barrier layers can be eliminated. In addition, polymer films, even of rigid, glassy materials, have considerably greater flexibility than sputtered metal or ceramic films. They are therefore much better-suited to flexible media applications than metal films.

The environmental stability of the ODI medium has been demonstrated in two types of experiments:

- Shelf-life studies in which the read/write characteristics of samples were determined as a function of accelerated environmental aging.

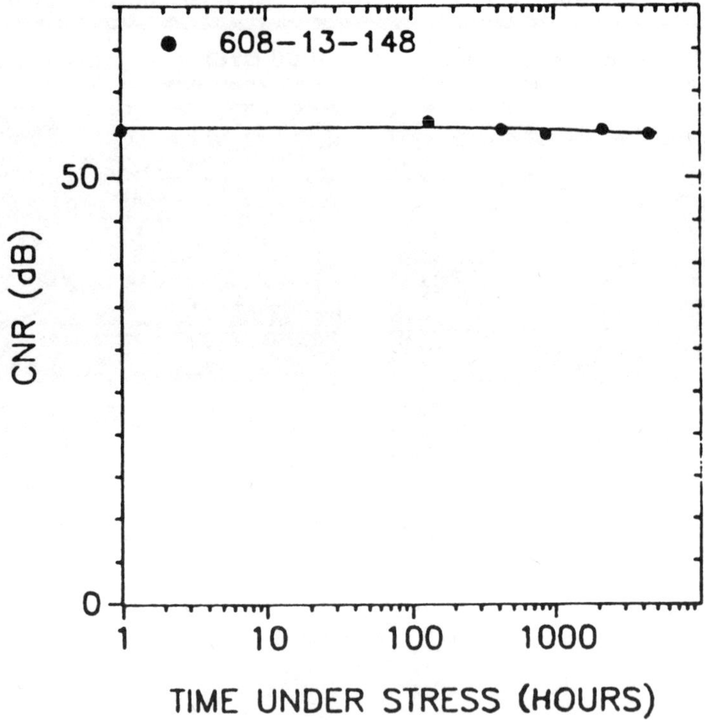

Figure 9. CNR After Environmental Exposure of Al Media at 60 degrees and 85 Percent Relative Humidity for About 6000 Hours. (Courtesy, ODI)

- Data integrity experiments in which data werewritten on virgin disks and then subjected to environmental stress to see what effect the stress would have on the written data.

The results of a typical accelerated shelf-life experiment are shown in Figure 9. Disks were subjected to accelerated aging at 60 degrees Centigrade and 85 percent Relative Humidity (RH). CNR was virtually unchanged after 6,000 hours of environmental exposure. In addition, microscopic examination of previously-written data indicated little or no change in the data after environmental exposure. Similarly, when data was written on a disk and then re-read after environmental exposure, no loss in data recovery was observed after 1,500 hours of exposure at 60 degrees Centigrade and 85 percent RH.

Advantages of ODI Medium

There are rather broad tolerances on the thicknesses of the expansion and retention layers because the constraints on layer thickness are mechanical rather than optical in the ODI air-incident medium. This simplifies process control and improves yields in the manufacturing process.

Secondly, current levels of media performance have been achieved using commercially-available resins and dyes.

Thirdly, the ODI medium is adaptable to new laser diode technology. As the wavelengths of laser diodes continue to decrease, the ODI medium can be adapted simply by changing the expansion or retention layer dye to absorb at the new wavelength. As wavelengths decrease into the visible range, the cost of the dyes will decrease significantly, and their stability will improve. In addition, the decrease in diffraction-limited spot size will allow increases in data density and sensitivity.

Fourthly, the structure is mechanically rugged. The retention layer consists of a tough abrasion-resistant glassy resin, while the expansion layer is a tough flexible elastomer. Both materials are well-adapted to use on a flexible substrate.

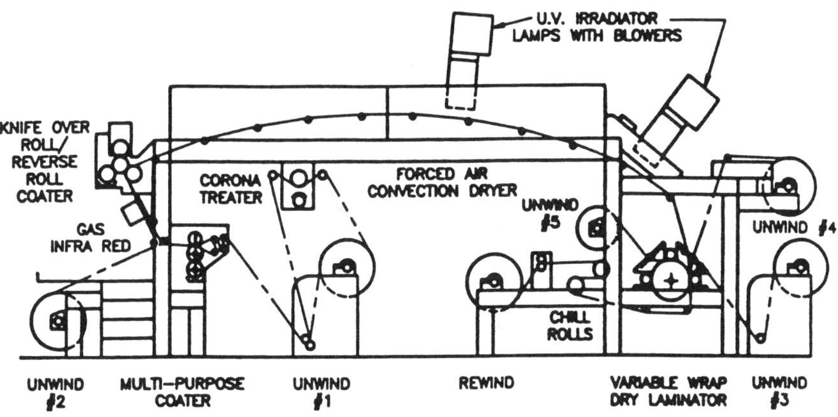

Figure 10. Pilot Coater/Laminator. (Courtesy, ODI)

Basic Web-Coating Technology

In most web-coating processes, a solution is transferred from a cylinder, called the coating roll, to a moving sheet of substrate which is unwound from a roll at one end of the machine and rewound onto another roll at the other end of the machine. The process is shown schematically in Figure 10. There are many different web-coating processes, but most differ only in:

- the manner by which the coating solution is applied to the coating roll
- the direction in which the coating roll rotates with respect to the motion of the substrate
- the method by which contact is maintained between the substrate and the coating roll

One common means of applying the coating solution to the coating roll is by means of a metering roll. Both the applicator roll and the metering roll are smooth cylinders, either metal or rubber-coated. Either the applicator roll or the metering roll rotates through a pan containing the coating solution. The gap setting and relative rotational speeds of the applicator roll and the metering roll determine the amount of solution which is applied to the moving web.

This type of coating process is referred to as a roll coating process. In knife-over-roll coating processes the coating solution is applied to the coating roll by a fountain or slot-die applicator. The coating thickness is then adjusted to the desired value by the coating knife, which wipes off excess coating solution before the coating cylinder is brought into contact with the web. In *gravure coating* the coating cylinder is engraved with a pattern of cells of different shapes and spacings. The cells are filled with coating solution as they rotate through the pan. Excess solution is wiped from the surface of the coating roll by the doctor blade. Solution is transferred to the web from the cells by differences in surface tension between the cylinder and the web. Since gravure processes offer the best control over coating thickness for solutions of low viscosity, our studies in optical media coating have centered on gravure processes.

Gravure processes are generally referred to as either *direct gravure* or *reverse gravure*. If the coating roll and the substrate are moving in the same direction, the process is referred to as *direct gravure*. If the coating roll is rotating in the opposite direction from the substrate, the process is referred to as *reverse gravure*. Processes in which the coating solution is picked up by one rotating cylinder and transferred to the coating roll are referred to as *offset gravure* processes. In direct gravure pressure is maintained between the web and the coating roll by means of a rubber-coated backing roll. In reverse gravure a backing roll may be used, but the web can also be wrapped over the coating roll by means of two idler rolls on either side of the coating roll. This latter technique is known as *kiss gravure*, and is used to minimize patterning due to imperfections in the backing roll. Reverse gravure was preferred with contact maintained by the kiss gravure method for most of ODI's coating experiments.

Web-Coating of the ODI Medium

Four series of coating experiments were carried out on two different coating machines to test the feasibility of coating the ODI medium on flexible substrates. A variety of resins and dyes were used in the expansion and retention layers to test both coating quality and media performance. Substrate thickness was varied from 48 gauge (typical of videotape products) to 300 gauge, which is the standard substrate for magnetic floppy disks. As the substrate thickness is decreased, the rotational speed required in the drive to achieve dynamic stabilization of the medium is reduced. As the rotational speed of the media decreases, sensitivity increases, allowing the use of lower-powered and less expensive laser diodes in the optical head. The majority of coatings were made on 142 gauge substrate. Little or no difference was observed in coating behavior as a function of substrate thickness. This indicates that the ODI medium may be adaptable to a variety of storage formats, including optical tape and cards as well as flexible and rigid optical disks.

Coating surface quality was evaluated by three methods:

- Differential Interference Contrast (DIC) microscopy
- Interferometry with a Kosaka HiPOSS interferometer
- Interferometry with a Wyko scanning interferometer

DIC microscopy revealed that the coatings were generally free from texture or phase separation. Both surface texture and average surface roughness (Ra) were determined using the Kosaka interferometer. A typical scan of the coating surface is shown in along with the frequency distribution of the defects observed. The surface roughness for the sample was 3.0nm. Surface defects were generally less than 10nm in height and radius, and thus are small compared to the dimensions of the data marks which are written on the medium. They will, therefore, contribute little to the noise floor of the medium. Data for surface roughness for all web-coated media samples are summarized in Table 1 along with data for three typical spin-coated samples. Surface roughness for the web-coated samples averaged 4.1nm with a range from 1.2nm to 19nm. The three spin-coated samples had an average surface roughness of 1.1nm with a range from 0.9nm to 1.5nm. Since the web-coated samples represented a wide range of coating conditions and resin systems, the average for the total sample population is somewhat broad. However, if the three worst coatings are removed from the sample population, the average surface roughness for the remaining fourteen samples decreases to 2.2nm with a range from 1.2nm to 4.4nm. These results are quite comparable to the

ODI MEDIA SAMPLES

		Ra(nm)	Peak-to Valley (nm)
Web-Coated Media			
	17 Samples	$\bar{x}$ = 4.1nm Range = 1.2 - 19nm	$\bar{x}$ = 71nm Range = 14 - 350nm
	14 Samples	$\bar{x}$ = 2.2nm Range = 1.2 - 4.4nm	$\bar{x}$ = 34nm Range = 14 - 90nm
Spin-Coated Media			
	3 Samples	$\bar{x}$ = 1.1nm Range = 0.9 - 1.5nm	$\bar{x}$ = 15nm Range = 12 - 18nm

Table 1. Surface Roughness of Web-Coated ODI Media Samples. (Courtesy, ODI)

spin-coated media samples, and indicate that web-coating can be used to coat the ODI medium.

Static and Dynamic Performance of Web-Coated ODI Media

Media marking thresholds for web-coated samples were determined using a static media tester. Reflectivity at 840nm was determined using a Perkin-Elmer Lambda 9 spectrophotometer with integrating sphere. Results are summarized in Table 2. Initial coatings had reflectivities of 6 to 7 percent at 840nm. Write thresholds were 100-120ns with a laser power of 10 mW at the media surface for the first detectable marks. In subsequent coating runs reflectivity was increased to 12 percent at 840nm, while mark thresholds were reduced to 30 to 40ns. Typical rigid air-incident ODI media has a threshold of 60 to 80ns and a reflectivity of 12 to 14 percent.

Since ODI's dynamic media tester is not fitted with a Bernoulli plate to stabilize the media, flexible samples had to be fixed to a rigid substrate prior to testing. This was accomplished by stretching the flexible samples over a hoop and then attaching the stretched film to a 120mm polycarbonate substrate. The resulting sample was flat enough to allow the focus servo in the dynamic tester to follow the surface of the media as it rotated.

The sample has a very sensitive marking threshold of approximately 2mW at 3m/s linear velocity. CNR increases rapidly with increasing write power, reaching 30dB at 3mW. As the write power is increased further, the carrier level continues to increase, but the noise floor increases as well. Mi-

Static Write Thresholds		
	Initial:	100 - 120ns at 10mW
	Current:	30 - 40ns at 10mW
Reflectivity		
	Initial:	6 - 7% at 840nm
	Current:	up to 12% at 840nm

Table 2. Performance of Web-Coated Samples. (Courtesy, ODI)

croscopic examination of the written marks as a function of write power indicates that marks written at higher write power (>7 mW) were ablative in nature. The increase in noise floor was due to the debris caused by the ablation of the retention layer. This indicates that the retention layer formulation used in these preliminary coating experiments needs to be improved. Media sensitivity, however, is comparable to or better than rigid media samples, and mark morphology at lower write power is very similar to rigid media. With improvements in coating quality and materials selection, flexible media performance should be comparable to rigid media.

Preformatting of flexible media will be required in order to achieve low media cost. ODI has conducted some preliminary experiments to determine whether preformat marks can be embossed directly onto the retention layer surface. A nickel-plated stamper similar to those used to injection mold rigid substrates was used as the embossing tool. The stamper was placed onto a special centering platen and preheated in a hydraulic press. A sample of flexible media was then placed into the press and the pressure was increased to approximately 500psi. When the sample was removed, the grooves from the stamper were clearly visible in the retention layer surface. Microscopic examination of the sample indicated that the groove structure was well-replicated, except for minor imperfections due to dust particles.

Conclusions from Preliminary Experiments

- Conventional gravure coating processes maintain adequate thickness control to allow web-coating of ODI optical media technology.

- Surface roughness of web-coated media is comparable to spin-coated media.

- Sensitivity of web-coated media is comparable to spin-coated media. Materials need to be improved to increase mark contrast and eliminate ablative marking on flexible media.

- Preliminary experiments indicate that preformat information can be embossed directly into the retention layer surface.

Plans for Commercialization of ODI Flexible Media

ODI has entered into a licensing agreement with Teijin Limited of Japan for the development of flexible optical media products using ODI technology. Teijin, Ltd. is currently conducting experiments in several areas. These include:

- Optimization of materials systems for:

  - increased media reflectivity
  - improved mark contrast and cycling performance
  - increased dye stability for improved shelf life and archival keeping

- Development of dynamic testing capability for flexible media

- Development of working relationships with drive manufacturers in the United States and Japan.

ODI expects that improvements in media performance will require twelve to eighteen months worth of work. Samples of flexible media for use by drive companies for drive development should be available by mid-1990. Pilot-scale quantities of media for beta-site testing should follow in early 1991. Drive development schedules are difficult to project, since drive partners have not been established. ODI expects, however, that drives for beta-site testing will be available by mid-1991; commercial drives available in limited quantities by early 1992. Form factor for the drive has not been determined. Either 89mm or 130mm formats would be possible. This would yield capacities of 100 to 600MBs of user data per side, depending upon the encoding scheme used.

Capital costs for media production are relatively low compared to those for injection-molded substrates with vacuum-deposited or spin-coated active layers. As a result, the disk cartridge will be one of the major cost items. Initial prices for media have not been determined, but should not exceed $50 per cartridge for single or double-sided media. As volume increases and yields improve, selling price of the media should decrease to $15 per cartridge. This will require approximately three years after commercial introduction.

Future Directions

While the first application of ODI media technology in flexible format will be as rotating disk media, other formats will be explored as well. Web-coated materials can be slit into optical tape or die-cut into optical data cards. Embossing technology can be used to preformat tape and cards, as well as providing the opportunity to include ROM data along with user-written data. Opportunities in both optical tape and optical data card will be explored by ODI and its licensees.

References

Halter, J.M. and Iwamoto, N.E. "Thermal-mechanical modeling of a reversible dye-polymer medium", pp. 201-210. IN: *SPIE Volume 899: Optical Storage Technology and Applications*, 1988.

Lind, M.A. and Hartman, J.S. "Performance of a reversible dye-polymer optical recording medium", pp. 211-218. IN: *SPIE Volume 899: Optical Storage Technology and Applications*, 1988.

Perera, S. Robert. "The Flexible Optical WORM Drive", presented at the Ninth Annual Optical Information Storage Conference, Hyatt Regency Hotel, Arlington, VA, Crystal City, September, 1989.

Pountain, D. "Digital Paper." *Byte*, February 1989: pp. 274-280.

Skiens, W.E. and Russell, G.A. "Rewritable dye-polymer optical storage medium: dynamic performance characteristics." IN: *Polymers in Information Storage Technology*, ACS Symposium Series, Washington, D.C., 1989.

5

End-User Requirements for Networking an Integrated Rewritable Workstation into a Professional Work Group

Mary Ann O'Connor

As companies go through the design and marketing of technology-related products, it remains a constant battle not to lose sight of a very simple marketing concept: "What end-user need does this product really satisfy?". The answer to this question is not always an easy one. Many times in the field of high technology, products are often looking for markets. Development almost always moves faster than user awareness and product and application developers continually find themselves in a position of having to educate our audience as to the benefits of our product. As many times as this effort works, it also fails. When it does not fail, the problem is not the inability to educate, but rather the ability to properly identify true user need. Sometimes the developer is lucky and the customer discovers what the product does on their own and finds the product is successful in spite of our efforts. That is, however, certainly not a position in which most product developers wish to find themselves.

Integrated workstations which utilize rewritable optical storage are available today. It is important to ask some very basic, but important, questions: Who are the end-users for these products?; What are their applications?; and, perhaps most importantly, What are their requirements?

This chapter will address some of these questions by examining the phases of evolution that end-user computing is currently going through and what this path of evolution means in terms of today's products. This chapter will also take a look at the dynamics and requirements of work group computing and how they conform with the applications for workstations utilizing rewritable optical storage.

The Phase of Computing

The Nolan Norton Institute specializes in studying personal computer utilization and productivity in corporations. They theorize that end-user computing evolves in phases, and these phases ultimately determine the return on investment that corporations realize from personal computing.

The first phase they identify is called "Technology Proficiency" during which time microcomputers first begin to enter an organization. During this phase, early adopters realize how to use microcomputers effectively. At this stage, however, there is little data concerning improved productivity or other benefits to the end-user.

The second phase identified by the Nolan Norton Institute is "Task Automation." This is when the microcomputer is focused on a specific task and that task is automated to some degree. Examples include spreadsheets for the task of calculations and word processors for typing tasks. These tasks are highly individualized and specific. During this phase, organizations begin to perceive the real benefits of personal computing. It is estimated that corporations double task efficiency during this phase. This could be a very significant point, considering most corporations are in this phase today.

Personal computing is just now moving into the third phase called "Process Automation" (sometimes referred to as "Office Integration"). During this phase, having experienced success with personal computers on an individual basis, companies begin to connect their organizations together by integrating groups of stand-alone computers. Often times this involves rethinking work processes and introducing such new concepts as electronic communications and electronic information sharing. It also involves certain new technologies such as networks, more powerful computers to be used as file servers, and high-capacity storage devices, including optical disks.

A key element in this third stage is a change in goals. Rather than improved efficiency as a goal, as was the case in phase two, the third phase seeks improved effectiveness. Usually, the way to become more effective is to change what the worker does rather than attempt to perform the same tasks faster. This is the first phase in personal computing that requires careful and thoughtful planning prior to implementation. *Organizations must be very careful to pay as much attention to work group dynamics and organizational structure during the planning of this phase as they do to the technologies required to implement it.*

The fourth and final phase identified by the Institute's study is "Business Transformation". Very few companies have ventured into this particular stage. Business Transformation occurs after work groups are connected and are operating effectively as independent units. This phase involves tying the entire organization together in much the same way that individual work groups are brought together. The larger the organization, the more difficult this task becomes because it truly involves changing the way companies (and individuals) conduct business. During this final phase, the best successes appear to be in small, startup organizations who are created with the concept of organizational automation in mind.

Given that "Process Automation" is the upcoming phase in personal computing, it may present the greatest opportunity for workstations utilizing rewritable optical storage. Understanding the requirements of work groups may be the key to successful marketing of rewritable optical products.

Work Group Requirements

First, it is important to understand the difference between departmental computing and work group computing. Departmental computing often has specific requirements related to the specialized functions of the department. These requirements may be best met by applications software and the corresponding hardware which may or may not include rewritable optical disk-based workstations. Work group computing, on the other hand, may involve the members of different departments but who have a need for some common functionality, including resource or data sharing.

Members of a work group have a strong need for individualization. This includes being able to select their workstation of choice (IBM, DEC, Macintosh, Sun) and their applications of choice. Members of a work group often do not wish to become computer experts.

Members of a work group also have an additional requirement for sophisticated communications. This includes electronic mail and messaging, centralized calendaring and scheduling, and the sharing of data. Members of a work group also have a need to share resources. These resources include such things as printers and plotters, storage devices, communications devices, and data.

In addition, there is a need to provide centralized control over certain functions within the group. These functions include backup of information (image and data) from the workstations or centralized file server, software distribution and system administration for qualified access as well as maximum performance and efficiency. There must also be a provision for growth and the management of unstructured information such as different file types.

Finally, no discussion of work group computing could be complete without addressing the needs of work product production. This statement refers to the integration of varied information types such as text, graphics, images, and maybe even voice. It also means providing tools to the work group which improve the quality of the content and output of work products. Examples of these tools include spelling checkers and other writing aids as well as desk-top publishing packages. Finally, because of increased interaction with other systems and work groups, there must be the ability to integrate (connect) with other information management systems, regardless of vendor.

In addition to the above requirements, the introduction of optical storage devices has created a new requirement; that is, the management and control of large amounts of complex data. Since rewritable optical storage provides the capability to store massive amounts of information from multiple users, and because there is a need to share that information among various users, there is a critical need to quickly and efficiently locate appropriate information in a fashion that makes it accessible to all the members of a work group. These characteristics of rewritable optical storage creates the demand for tools and processes which properly store and retrieve data using methods intuitive to all work group members. Examples will be discussed in more detail later in this chapter.

Work group computing encompasses several technologies: workstations, networks, optical technology, facsimile, modems, and other peripherals. Simply attaching a new device, such as an optical disk to any of the workstations or servers may not be the solution to a problem. In fact, it may, create problems of its own.

Applications of Rewritable Storage

This section will examine some of the ways in which rewritable optical storage is being currently used and various plans for its application. A basic comparison of these uses with the requirements for work group computing will be offered.

The first and most obvious use is for mass storage of information. Mass storage means being able to maintain vast amounts of data online. This could be in the case of an individual, but certainly appears to be very practical when considering the needs of a group of users who find it necessary to share data.

Another application is backup. Permanent backup (or archive) also implies data from multiple users as opposed to an individual. It also appears to be most cost-effective for optical media in specialized situations, given other, less costly alternatives, such as tape and DAT.

Temporary backup can mean making copies of specific files on an individual's PC and storing those files in a central location, such as a server equipped with rewritable optical storage, to protect those files from accidental damage. This process is typically repeated at regular intervals and only involves storage of the latest version of specific files.

Image management is an application which transcends many industries and, perhaps, provides the greatest opportunity for rewritable optical storage-based workstations. Up until recently, image management has involved a single dedicated workstation which, because of the size of image files, usually involves some sort of optical storage device.

Due to the desire to share image data in work group environments, systems are now emerging which include the ability to transfer images across networks. There are some inherent performance issues associated with transferring large image files across a network which are now being addressed by a variety of vendors utilizing an assortment of solutions.

An extension of the image management application is vertical market applications. Examples of these are litigation support systems, insurance processing, personnel records systems, and banking applications. These systems combine image management capabilities with specialized vertical market software to provide a total solution, often involving sharing of information across multiple workstations.

The next category of applications is called "Specialty Applications" and is a catch-all category. Utilizing a workstation equipped with rewritable optical storage for CD-ROM preparation and other information publishing activities is an example of a specialty application. Although information distribution using rewritable optical disks has not yet been attempted, this is certainly a viable alternative for internal corporate distribution of information, particularly when dealing with large volumes of highly confidential information.

The last category of applications is called "Groupware" for lack of a better term. The best way to describe groupware is through a specific product example.

OfficeWorks from NBI combines a number of hardware and software components to provide a total solution product for work group computing. The hardware elements include a variety of workstations, with networking and other communications capabilities, and the potential for optical storage.

The software aspects of OfficeWorks provide an amazingly rich set of functions which address the needs of work groups.

File Management

The file management applications includes Electronic Index Cards, Revision Managements Services, Document Templates and the Global File System.

Electronic Index Cards allows a user to attach procedural and descriptive information to MS-DOS, Microsoft Windows, Macintosh, UNIX or OA-

Sys (dedicated word processing) files. These files may include all file types including text, graphics, sound, and image. Index cards can then be used to search, sort and retrieve files, including online, archived or hard copy paper files. This is particularly useful in optical disk environments where more files than ever before are being stored on a single disk. It also allows for the merging of electronic and non-electronic information without having to go through the difficulties of conversion to electronic media.

Keeping track of the most up-to-date version of a document, spreadsheet, image, or other file can be a difficult task, especially when several members of a work group are involved in its development. The task is even more difficult when the document or file must undergo many revisions and multiple levels of approval. Optical storage allows (perhaps for the first time) the storage of multiple versions of a document, and the graphics and/or illustrations associated with it. This complex capability, however, requires a tool such as Revision Management Services to control the revision process by maintaining and tracking multiple revision levels of both the document and its associated graphics. This allows the various members of a work groups to process and revise their portions of the document without worrying about which version they may be working on and who else might be making changes as well.

Document Templates is a procedural processing tool that allows users to create specially tailored procedures for handling frequently used documents or files such as memos, proposals, spreadsheets, and special reports. With this tool, pre-set formats for documents and files can be established, along with specific tracking of information to be listed on the documents' Electronic Index Card. Then, users can simply select the template established for a particular format, and the system will automatically display the appropriate Index Card for fill-in and then create the document format. This process saves time and ensures consistency of file format and handling within a work group. It also can control where a file is stored within a complex network that contains a variety of storage devices in a variety of locations. For example, automatic archiving to a server-based optical disk can be a procedure assigned to a specific file type to ensure its storage integrity and accessibility by other work group members. Certain files types (memos, reports) could also contain automatic routing to specific members of the work group to increase communications capabilities.

The Global File System provides network-wide access to public files on servers and individual PCs within a network regardless of the type of storage device which is contained on that server or workstation. This System not only provides access to all storage devices on the network, but also presents those files to the user in a familiar interface, for example, MS-DOS, Windows, and Macintosh.

Information Management

NBI's information management applications offer far more than just the ability to find information.

Information management becomes a complex task when multiple members of a work group or individuals in different work groups are involved. These individuals are probably using different (and incompatible) systems and different software packages. Moreover, work group members have a need to develop final products that incorporate text, data, graphics, and increasingly, images. Work group members often work on pieces of a project separately, merging the pieces in the final stage of review and approval. Two examples of this type of working environment are research organizations and technical documentation departments. These work groups contain writers (authors), graphics designers, technical assistants, technical reviewers, and support personnel (who often do the final assembly).

The Content Retrieval System allows users to retrieve documents even when they have minimal information about the documents. It is a full text retrieval package that searches by content rather than name. This capability is particularly useful in environments where previously created information can be edited and reused over and over again, such as in proposals and grant requests.

BRS/Search provides a structured environment for full text retrieval of information and allows for various searches by key-word indexes.

Revisable Document Interchange is NBI's file translation software which provides translation between twenty-five different word processing formats and a number of PC to Macintosh file conversions as well. It allows users of different systems (hardware and software) to share and exchange data.

UNIFY is a powerful relational database and ACCELL is an integrated application development environment. They allow the development of custom applications and information handling systems which are optimized to a particular work groups processes and requirements.

When work group members are involved in electronic transfer and the sharing of information through complex systems, there are some basic administrative capabilities which ensure data integrity and security and allow them to interact with the system in a transparent way. Typically, these capabilities are provided through the services of a System Administrator who should be able to interact with the system and provide services to its users without extensive technical knowledge and skill. Examples of these services include automatic backup of data and management of the systems resources.

Other capabilities which should be included in an effective work group environment are Electronic Mail and Messaging as well as Time Management and Resource Scheduling. These applications take advantage of the systems integration within each workstation and provide key time-saving capabilities for each work group member.

Having examined a specific software offering for work group productivity, it is important to return to the original listing of work group requirements and see how the various technologies and applications, available today, address these needs.

As Figure 1 illustrates, *no one* single application or technology addresses all the requirements of work group computing. In fact, it requires a tightly

REQUIREMENTS	APPLICATIONS	TECHNOLOGY
NEED FOR INDIVIDUALIZATION		
WORKSTATION OF CHOICE		VARIOUS PCs
APPLICATIONS OF CHOICE		WORKSTATIONS
MINIMAL EXPERTISE (EASE OF USE)	GROUPWARE	GROUPWARE
COMMUNICATION		NETWORK
MAIL/MESSAGING	E-MAIL	WORKSTATIONS
CALENDARING & SCHEDULING	GROUPWARE	
DATA SHARING		OPTICAL STORAGE
CONTROL		NETWORK
BACKUP		OPTICAL STORAGE
ACCESS (SECURITY)		
PERFORMANCE & EFFICIENCY		
SOFTWARE DISTRIBUTION		
GROWTH		OPTICAL STORAGE
MANAGEMENT OF UNSTRUCTURED DATA	GROUPWARE	
SHARED RESOURCES		NETWORK
PRINTERS		
STORAGE		OPTICAL STORAGE
COMMUNICATIONS		
DATA		OPTICAL STORAGE
WORK PRODUCT PRODUCTION		
INTEGRATION OF VARIED INFO TYPES	IMAGE MANAGEMENT	OPTICAL STORAGE
TOOLS	SPECIALTY	
INTEGRATION WITH OTHER SYSTEMS		

Figure 1. A Comparison of Work Group Requirements with Applications and Technology. (Courtesy, Compact Discoveries, Inc.)

integrated, well-orchestrated combination of hardware and software which can be tailored to the general and specific needs of a particular group.

Conclusion

In conclusion, organizations wishing to capitalize on the Process Automation phase of personal computing should pay close attention to the first three phases of end-user computing — Technology Proficiency, Task Automation, and Process Automation. Organizations should ensure that adequate, up-front planning has gone into the design of a work group solution and that there has not been an overemphasis on technology alone.

The solution should provide for a smooth and elegant integration of the various components necessary for work group computing. Simply attaching components without regard to their intended interaction and use by the work group will lead to complex and confusing systems which users will then refuse to incorporate into their work processes. The NBI approach to work group computing (see Figure 2) illustrates what this chapter refers to as "an elegant integration of components."

Finally, despite their apparent similarities, every work group is unique and has specific requirements all their own. Any system must be tailorable to these requirements and should be able to change and grow with the group.

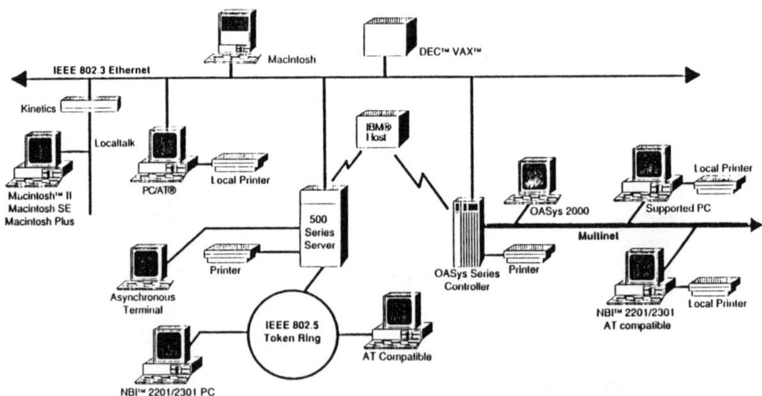

Figure 2. An example of an integrated work group solution. Rewritable optical disk can be added to any workstation or server depending upon application requirements. (Courtesy, NBI.)

6
Integrated Rewritable Optical Storage Workstations: An End-User's Perspective

Otmar Foelsche

In contrast to purely magnetic media, optical media is fully and easily transportable. Easily transported, it is not subject to the perils of magnetic fields, atmospheric conditions, electric fields and other hazards. Therefore, it may be considered a relatively safe distribution medium for data of any kind, application, text, graphics, and sound.

Optical rewritable media are superior to write-once (WORM) and CD-ROM because it offers the user the ability to distribute large amounts of data with a built-in capability for updating directly to the same storage medium; that is, an existing data set on a rewritable optical medium can be updated daily via a network. For purposes of updating, CD-ROMs have to be replaced (an expensive proposition for seller and buyer) and write-once optical disks would also have to be replaced (an even more expensive proposition) when they are loaded to capacity (up to a gigabyte per disk side).

Current low-end rewritable optical drives and disks in mass production use double-sided 280-megabyte rewritable optical media on single-sided drives. Thus, the maximum amount of storage directly accessible to the user (i.e. without disk swapping) is approximately 260MBs. Drive access time is significantly slower than that of a similar-sized magnetic device in the 300MB range.

This chapter focuses on the possible utilization of rewritable optical storage in the humanities with special reference to the areas of foreign/second language instruction. Products currently under development in this area may have a significant impact on research and instruction in these areas as well as foreign/second language publications, correspondence, translations, and training.

Workstation Requirements

Workstation descriptions in the humanities, particularly in languages, represent the ever-increasing thirst for higher speed, more storage, and more sophisticated computer capabilities. Ten years ago, a word processing workstation capable of displaying and printing almost all characters and diacritics of the Roman alphabet was a dream. Today, at the cutting edge, word processing is the lowest capability of such a workstation, while accessing the entire reference room (and possibly all other holdings) of a university library is now the dream.

A proposal for a Language Workstation, developed by David Bantz and the author, was proposed in an internal proposal in the fall of 1987. This proposal mentioned optical storage media for the storage of texts, reference materials, sounds, and visuals. In the following year, this original proposal was expanded. The Consortium for Language Teaching and Learning provided funds to continue the investigation into the feasibility of a language workstation jointly with Brown and Harvard University. At the time this chapter was being written, this proposal was in the process of being rewritten to reflect discussions, research and development of the last year (1989). Optical rewritable storage media could play a significant role in the development of the first fully functional version of this workstation. Indeed, they already play a role in the development of various workstation modules.

Research and development of these various modules normally begins with the design, mockup, and prototyping of small but fully functioning applications which are to be integrated later into the complete environment of a workstation. In some cases, the existence of a small but fully functioning application leads to immediate demand by users in the academic community and requires the production of fairly large datasets. These datasets are changed and adjusted as groups of people deal simultaneously with pedagogical issues, interface design, code streamlining, and marketing decisions. The safety and integrity of existing data in this ongoing process is uppermost in the minds of project managers.

Case Example: Brown, Harvard, Dartmouth Language Workstation

A typical example of this process is the current production of the Hanzi Assistant, destined to be published and marketed as a CD-ROM and also targeted as an integral part of the Chinese area in the Brown, Harvard, Dartmouth Language Workstation. Approximately one dozen individuals worked on this project during the academic year 1988 to 1989.

Project managers faced the problem of having to control and safeguard very large amounts of data from various sources in various formats:

1. Approximately 4500 brush stroke images had to be produced by a calligrapher on 8.5 x 11-inch sheets of paper. All 4500 images had to be scanned in individually as MacPaint files, named, and provided with translations and so-called disambiguation tables for homonyms.

2. Approximately 4500 traced brush stroke images had to be produced by several students and stored on disk as animation files.

3. Approximately 3000 individual pronunciation files for male and female voices had to be digitized from a tape made abroad and put on disk as resource files.

4. Close to 10,000 translations, several thousand Pinyin transcriptions, and character data (number of strokes) had to be combined with the files created in 1, 2, and 3.

The initial production phase requires the assemblage of complete demonstrations sets combining 1 through 4. The final production phase will require adjustments and additions on almost all image and animation files. Pre-pressing debugging and testing will require moving and duplicating files totalling about 150MBs each. This would normally require several huge hard disks, each holding one dataset. It would also require tape back-up units to satisfy minimal demands of data security. Optical rewritable drives would allow the storage of several generations of data in a possibly more secure medium than that of a hard disk, magnetic tape, or floppy disk.

With insufficient funding for two rewritable optical disks, we plan to use a combination of hard disks and optical rewritable disks to produce the final data for the pressing of the CD-ROM disc. It is expected that this combination of storage devices will satisfy several requirements: several easily accessible complete backups, and adjustments on third and fourth duplicates of the complete set, keeping the original set fully intact in case disaster strikes.

After receiving our drive, we found the accompanying manual poorly written and ill-adapted for the Macintosh environment. The formatting software itself appeared to be a "pre-beta" release, and comprehensible only to experienced Macintosh users with some high-level hard disk experience.

Nevertheless, we managed to get the drive running and function appropriately. While the software has been upgraded several times since, the manual has not. The rewritable optical disk received with the drive developed media problems on one side which made it impossible to write files beyond a certain size (between 60 and 80k). The rewritable optical disk was exchanged by the vendor and the replacement disk has been working correctly. Our second disk, however, refuses to write files beyond 40MBs on one side; the other side is fine.

Despite assistance and assurances from the vendor, we have not yet been able to install the rewritable optical drive as an Appleshare device. Presently, it is a SCSI device on one of our Macintosh II workstations. The rewritable optical drive, however, has not been totally reliable since it bombs fairly often on large backups from hard disks. The fact that the drive is working well on one side of a disk and not on the second side indicates the existence of an alignment problem. In general, we believe that we are victims of "juvenile" software, rather than of a questionable technology. We fully expect to use the drive for its intended purpose when a more mature version of the software is available.

This rewritable optical drive will be used to simulate the CD-ROM environment. This should allow the testing of the complete dataset on one side of the rewritable optical disk and the use of the second side of the disk as backup. Since the rewritable optical medium is faster than a CD-ROM drive and slower than a hard disk, acceptable feedback should be gleaned from our test concerning data access and sound access speeds. Last but not not least, the rewritable optical medium is expected to serve as the transportation medium to the CD-ROM manufacturing/replication facility.

Keeping our basic datasets on a rewritable optical medium will also allow us to perform several updates already in the planning stage and transfer them again to CD-ROM manufacturing facility without concern for the safety of the data.

Additional Applications and Functionas of the Language Workstation

Another Language Workstation area in which rewritable optical media may be used is electronic texts, glossaries, reference works, and dictionaries. At the moment, it is easy to imagine storing extensive electronic text libraries on rewritable optical media as well as on CD-ROM. Since CD-ROM production costs for large numbers are extremely low, we can safely assume that CD-ROM will serve as a delivery vehicle for texts, graphics, and sounds for the language workstation. CD-ROM represents the frozen state of data or scientific accomplishment. Rewritable optical media represents ongoing research, adjustable, manipulable data, ever-changing output, the last stage before actual CD-ROM manufacturing and replication.

Typically, dictionaries and reference works are outdated at the moment of publication. A specific edition of a drama by Shakespeare or a novel by Pasternak are final and definitive. They need not be ever changed. Glossaries and footnotes may be changed and expanded over time.

The Language Workstation needs definitive text, dictionary and reference works. What it needs most, however, is a storage medium that is easily updatable and transportable to allow one scientist in one institution to cooperate with another scientist in a different institution using the same large datasets.

Dictionary production, for example, depends on complex analysis of a corpus of words (the more the better) and the production of lists. In most cases, bilingual dictionaries are glossaries providing lists of equivalents. What is needed is contextual/collocational analysis and some kind of "knowledge processor" linking lists of two monolingual dictionaries. Prior to the availability of a rewritable optical disk-based workstation, this type of analysis could only be accomplished on mainframe computers because of the enormous storage requirements for these long lists. Optical rewritable media can satisfy these requirements to a very high degree allowing the processing of a corpus on a fast desktop machine.

Despite the fact that many dictionaries will be delivered on CD-ROM discs or as WORM media to the Language Workstation, dictionaries should be copied onto rewritable optical disks for on-the-spot updates. This task should be accomplished by directly incorporating updates and additions within the actual dictionary file. This process would allow a complete "user-specific" dictionary or reference work that consists of commercially available data integrated with user-generated data and possible updates and additions by colleagues and services in the same profession.

Since the Language Workstation provides texts and reference works and activities for the user (practicing, listening, reading, writing and combinations thereof) and language production (word processing and authoring), it is the combination, the synthesis, and the storage of a new effort which opens up new vistas. For example, the side-by-side reading of two critical editions with simultaneous production of a third critical edition commenting on both is now possible.

In language instruction, the multi-sensory or multidimensional activity, presentation, or investigation is far superior in producing results to the "flat" approach which depends on reading a book, or listening to tapes. The combination of computers with tape recorders for the purpose of teaching listening comprehension interactively is made unnecessary because large-capacity, rewritable optical media could store hours of digitized sound files, making the inconvenience of complex set-ups of recorders and computers superfluous. In this case we would be able to examine the combination of data existing in other media (probably CD-ROM) and integrate it with user-produced data on an optical rewritable disk for the purpose of writing, testing, and instructing.

As wonderful as video can be in any area of instruction, simple animation can amplify a point, or strengthen a concept without the clutter of the full, and sometimes distracting, "charged" video image. In many languages, verbs are used depending on whether they present dynamic or static concepts. A collection of simple, but alterable, animation sequences could support an instructor's efforts to develop models and sequences in instruction. Many of these models would not necessarily have to be language specific. A bus running from point A to point B would be at home in many cultures and languages. For example, generic sets of animations and pictures of objects could easily be produced on optical media from many other sources when storage space is virtually unlimited.

In culture and civilization courses, optical rewritable media may be considered alternatives to Laserdiscs™ such as interactive videodiscs. Whereas Laserdiscs can only display low-resolution NTSC color images, optical rewritable media can store high-resolution digitized color images in 8-, 14-,24-, or even 32-bit color resolution. Pictures of this quality require tremendous amounts of storage space. A Laservision™ disc can handle approximately 54,000 images on one side, while rewritable optical media can handle 250 to 1,000 8-bit images. Nevertheless, the capability of carrying about 500 high-resolution color images a rewritable optical disk opens up great possibilities. For example, a workstation could easily contain high-resolution color image libraries of the complete paintings of Caspar David Friedrich or Vincent van Gogh.

User Interface

The present interface prototype of the Language Workstation (see Figure 1) illustrates some of the functionalities described above. A Shakespeare text, a bilingual dictionary/glossary, and a video picture are visible; text can also be selected. Accompanying video, or audio alone belonging to the selected portion, can be produced by clicking on the appropriate icons. This environment could also be used by a student for essay writing; for example, the student could quote from the "hot" Shakespeare text so that the professor can read the student's point with the accompanying video or audio selections. The usefulness of such work has not yet been tested. There is, however, great potential in this type of application.

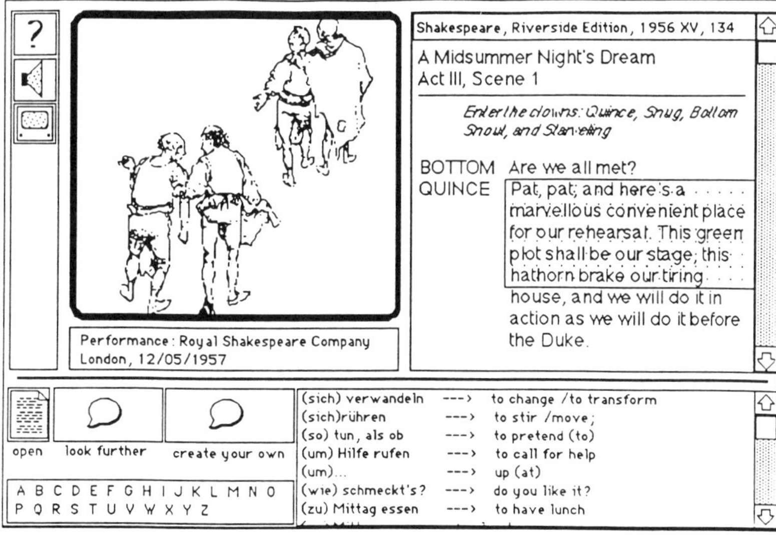

Figure 1. (Courtesy Language Resource Center, Dartmouth College)

Conclusion

Steve Jobs, founder of NeXT, Inc., has stated the interesting idea that optical rewritable media could serve as storage for a whole university education. With ever-increasing capabilities, this concept could be easily expanded to contain the entire life of a inidividual with sounds, photographs, education, and memorabilia.

The small but very important drawback concerns copyright. Recently, a few publishers expressed a certain willingness to allow researchers to deal with their materials, particularly dictionaries.

Other publishers have been adament in refusing to let anybody come close to their data. These publishers are missing the point. The future value of reference works lies in their accessibility and upgradability by the user and the publisher. Their value will also be determined by how easily they can be connected to other works for the purpose of research and production. Rewritable optical media appears to be the ideal medium for storing sizeable databases to which new data may be added constantly. Building flexible reference works and dictionaries on these media makes intellectual and economic sense.

Publishers should consider innovative billing practices for these types of databases. One suggestion would be offer a "give and take" similar to the way electric companies run meters of cogenerators in reverse when receiving electricity from them. A publisher could reduce charges on updates if users transmit useful data to publishers. Ted Nelson's Xanadu Project plans to bill for data according to whether it has just been seen, downloaded, or quoted and reprinted.

Another approach could be Denis Devlin's (Dartmouth College) Key-Server. Accordingly, the user would have all data under personal control but sophisticated access would only be possible through the ownership of a "key." This "key" would be available on the network and could serve as a billing device. A publisher could sell ten "access applications" and be assured that no more than ten users would simultaneously use the data at any time. Time used on the complete database could then be billed.

Rewritable optical media, once they are totally reliable, will probably be in high use in academia and industry within the next four years. Their storage capacity and their speed will probably increase dramatically. Although their application in academia has only been explored to a small extent, we can expect to see considerable innovative and extremely useful applications in the near future with rewritable optical storage.

7
Surrogate Manipulation: Early Experiences with the NeXT Computer in a University Research Enviornment

Joan Sustik Huntley and Michael Partridge

Once totally disparate commodities, the distinctions between computers and art, blur as they fuse together. Free associations with the word "computers" twenty years ago were "huge," 'heavy," "exorbitant," and "number crunching" — at best, the subject of artistic derision. A decade later, perceptions changed to "big," "bulky," "expensive," "word processing," and "databases" — useful to museum staffs. Today, the computer is recognized as "lightweight," "portable," "affordable," and a "multimedia development" platform perceived as an increasingly indispensable tool for the artist. Currently, computer software for art is designed for those who need information about art such as: librarians, museum curators, and for those who create art, the artists themselves. Typically, however, a given software program benefits only one population.

This need not be the case. In a project underway at the Computer-Assisted Instruction (CAI) Lab at the University of Iowa, we believe that it is not only possible, but indeed desirable, to create computer software useful to several populations working with art. Using a NeXT computer, we are developing "Fluxbase," an application that blends traditional capabilities with new functions, that defies categorization as a "database," "word processor," or "drawing tool," and that meets the needs of many groups interested in contemporary art.

This chapter was originally published as an article in the Summer 1990 issue of Multimedia Review (Meckler Corporation, Westport, CT) under the title: Fluxbase: A Virtual Exhibit.

From Where Do We Speak?

Multiple, non-standard cataloging systems are used in museums and libraries to control information about alternative contemporary art. While accommodating the needs of curators and librarians, these systems fail to adequately represent the artist's intentions. In April 1989, Estera Milman, Curator of the Alternative Traditions in Contemporary Arts Archive at the University of Iowa, organized a planning conference, sponsored by the National Endowment for the Arts, to address problems with existing art networks and information systems. Based on our earlier work with videodisc-based computer systems for traditional Western art, we were invited to design a prototype to suggest how technology can help solve this problem.

Questions Guiding Our Design

Traditional architecture software was used as a design metaphor. A "contractor's special" is a common, no frills, generalized blueprint, yielding look-alike houses in many suburban subdivisions. This approach is easy and inexpensive, but fails to produce the best design for either the physical location or the building's inhabitants. By contrast, architecture's "built to specification" is created with both the environment and inhabitants in mind. The same is true in designing computer-based programs. A program should be designed with the best fit for both the environment and consumers as well as the various of uses to be made of the program. In doing so, four questions guided the system design.

How Do Needs Of Contemporary Art Collections Differ?

Indexing methods and retrieval designs should reflect the structure of the collection they embody. The specific subset of contemporary art used in this prototype is known as "Fluxus." What is "Fluxus?" Definition and "Fluxus" are contradictory terms. It is impossible to state precisely when it started, or who was in it, or even what art it was. The fall 1979 issue of *lightworks* introduces Fluxus as:

> "Fluxus is a sort of alchemy. A box of broken watches, a deck of cards (each a two of spades), a concert performance of French Horns filled with Ping-pong balls. It is the act and transformation of life into art... Be it performance art, the construction of boxes, the publishing, the festivals, this is a thoughtful and life-giving art... Yet no one is quite sure how to reckon with Fluxus, and the critics and the scholars have, for the most part, avoided doing so. Possibly because it is sim-

ply not one thing. The contents and form and contributors are diverse and disunited as the paradoxes are plentiful. Fluxus has no manifesto. It was hardly even a movement and Peter Frank aptly labels it a tendency. To be sure, it coalesced artists, designers, chemists, engineers, writers and more from all parts of the world in the early 1960's...is seminal in the development of happenings and performance art, concept art, artists' publishing, correspondence art and more.Ultimately Fluxus is renegade art, always on the fringe and continually defying tradition."

What, then, are the distinguishing aspects of Fluxus that should be addressed in our technological response? Let us examine the work "Projects Class" by David Askevold (ed.) as an example.

Collaboration Among Artists

Flux artists collaborated significantly more than traditional artists. The collaborative tendency called for the artists to work together on individual artworks. "Projects Class" was a creation by 12 artists, each contributing a different card to the set. "Flux Year Box 2," the focal piece of our project, has at least seventeen contributing artists. Thus, this NeXT-based program needs to provide easy access to information about the multiple artists associated with a given work.

Understanding The Context

Many works of art are best understood in the context of the environment in which it was created, for example, politics, religion, or even the artist's personal history such as their physical and emotional states. Since Fluxus was a tendency rather than a well-defined movement, it is especially important to understand the events and environments in which Flux pieces were created. For example, in his article "Fluxus in New York, Peter Frank relates:

> "Higgins remembers Canal Street in the late 1950's and early 60's as an exciting, dynamic environment. The surplus stationers that predominated on the stretch of Canal between Centre Street and West Broadway were going out of business, and plastic surplus merchants and job lot dealers were replacing them. The little machines and objects available in these junk stores fascinated the artists in the neighborhood, including Higgins, Knowles, Lette Eisenhauer, and several Japanese including Ay-O, Yoko Ono, and Chieko Shiomi. It can be demonstrated

> that the visual aesthetic informing Fluxus work depends heavily on the *objet trouve* sensibility nurtured by the Canal Street atmosphere."

Experiential As Well As Observational

Some art is best appreciated when visually observed in two dimensions, such as the Mona Lisa. Three-dimensional art is often best appreciated when touched, or when the viewer moves around it such as a Henry Moore sculpture or when the viewer moves within it, for example, Chartres Cathedral. Still other art is best appreciated when the viewer manipulates it, and experiences its three dimensional unfolding over time In "Projects Class," it would be intriguing to see the results of the projects and the photographs and texts reordered as instructed, not just the instructions alone.

Several notable computerized databases embody these requirements. The most famous example of fluid and graceful control of a three-dimensional object is the "Greek Vases" videodisc at the Getty Museum of Art. At the University of Iowa, a HyperCard stack controlling a videodisc with 35,000 art images has been developed in which the user can zoom in progressively closer to view a painting, rotate a piece of sculpture, and move across an architectural site. Over a decade ago the MIT's Architecture Machine Group demonstrated "surrogate travel" through Aspen Colorado. None of these projects, however, embodied the sense of vicarious manipulation, the "virtual reality" component, users ought to experience when they open up Flux Year Box 2 and play with its contents.

Material Relative To The Works

Many Flux pieces were described on paper and then later produced from the descriptions, often by someone other than the artist; "Projects Class" is an example. These were created with such frequency that they acquired a name of their own: "artist's descriptions." Furthermore, since Flux works are contemporary creations, more printed information about the works (written by someone other than the artist) than exists, for example, about a work by Michelangelo. Thus the system must incorporate both types of information: graphic and encoded via a bit-mapped file or an analogue video signal, and ASCII text.

Characteristics such as greater artist collaboration, a need to know the context, the amount of graphic and textual material related to an artwork do occur in traditional art forms, but they are far more prominent in Fluxus. It is an issue of magnitude, of the degree to which these features occur, rather than whether they exist at all. If a characteristic of an object in a database occurs once in three thousand instances, the computer may not need to accommodate it. If the feature occurs in 2,500 of 3,000 objects, then the system design should reflect it.

Why Automate an Information Database in the Contemporary Arts?

Our original charge was to create a system that would rectify the discrepancies between the diverse indexing methods used by librarians, museum conservators, and archivists. For these people, the primary reason to automate is to gain more and better *information* about the works of art, as well as easier access to this information. Types of questions that could be answered include:

- did George Macunias create artist's books?
- where and when has a given artwork been exhibited / performed?
- where are artworks located today?
- which works of art sold for more than $50,000?
- how has the average price of artist's books changed over the past five years?

Solving this problem requires that the various parties maintaining information databases agree to a common set of data fields, terminology to define these fields, and protocols by which to share this information among the diverse systems that exist or will be created in the future. These are not trivial problems. Modifying a system that already exists may require changes in software and publications, new staff training, and last, but far from least, compromising on the the form and function of the various fields of the information database.

Many of the indexing systems and guidelines already in place have been thoughtfully conceived and well-executed. Some examples are the *Processing Manual* for the Franklin Furnace—a notable archive in New York, and the fields and procedures established by the Library of Congress. Yet, despite the richness of these adopted methods, they are dissimilar and in certain ways fail to capture the uniqueness of the artworks themselves.

As we became more familiar with contemporary art, especially Fluxus, it became clear that the discrepancy between the form in which information was stored or retrieved and the spirit of the artists caused a greater problem. Describing non-traditional artwork in traditional data structures obscured much of its identity. Expanding the database to include graphic and audio data, and to make this data available in a participatory rather than a read-only form, we needed to create a program that provided not only information about, but also an *understanding of*, an appreciation for the art. Questions which could then be answered include:

- how did the artists performance sound?
- what does an artwork located across the continent look like?
- how did the piece work?

In short, experimenting with multimedia representations could yield a greater understanding of the artworks than restricted, textual data fields; its need is fairly obvious in the title of a 1984 exhibit catalog from Toronto's Art Metropole: *evidence of the avant garde since 1957: selected works from the collection of art metropole including audio tapes, records, videotapes, film, multiples, kitsch, manuscripts, stamps, buttons, flyers, posters, correspondence, catalogues, porn, t-shirts, postcards, drawings, poems, mailers, books, photographs and ephemera.*

Whose Needs Are We Serving?

Librarians, curators, and archivists were well served by the original indexing system. Contemporary artists, however, also attended the NEA planning session. We believed it was necessary to also consider the interests and needs of contemporary artists, professors, students, curators, and librarians. Thus, we identified the following populations that varied in quality and quantity of their background knowledge; whether or not they wanted to correct, confirm or amplify the information; and whether or not they desired to have a more direct, experiential involvement with the art:

- administrator of an archive or library
- scholar / professor
- student
- original artist
- the community of artists

What Universe Are We Modelling?

Having recognized potential users, the universe that was of greatest interest:

- administrator of an archive: the local collection
- scholar / professor: worldwide collection
- student: the tendency in general and the artist in particular
- original artist: their own works
- the community of artists: works in the same genre

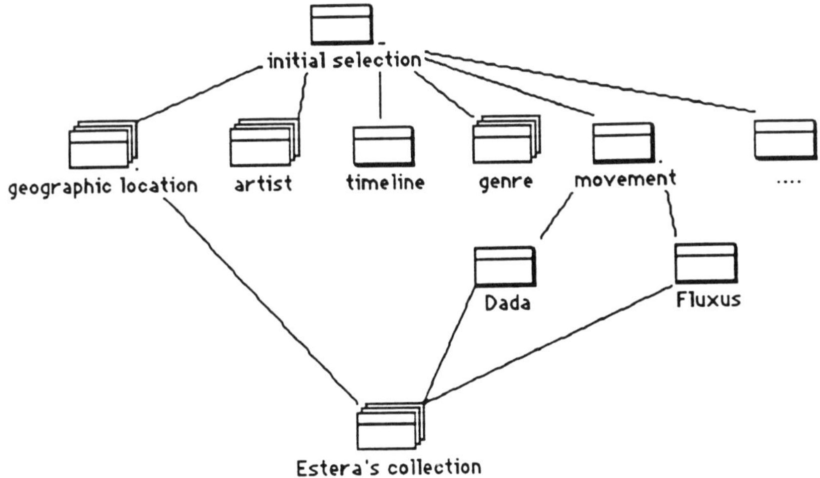

Implementing the Design

Given that Fluxus has an international tendency, and that Flux art exists in collections all over the world, the system was designed to lallow users to select artworks through several different conceptual entrances:

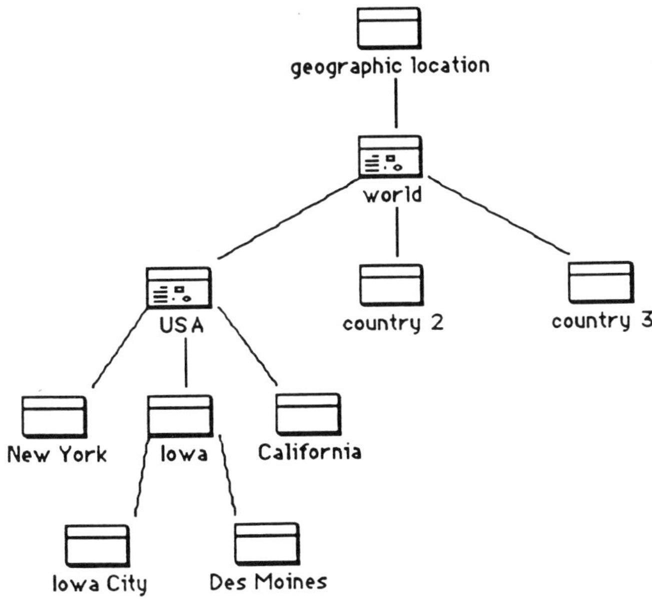

For example, using either traditional cartographic maps, or photographic clusters for the varying regions in the world, users will be able to select a geographic region. Since numerous networked computers were envisioned, users can narrow their visit to a single collection, one located in New York, for example, while they are in Los Angeles, and create a sort of virtual browsing.

Alternatively, they may have a particular artist already in mind:

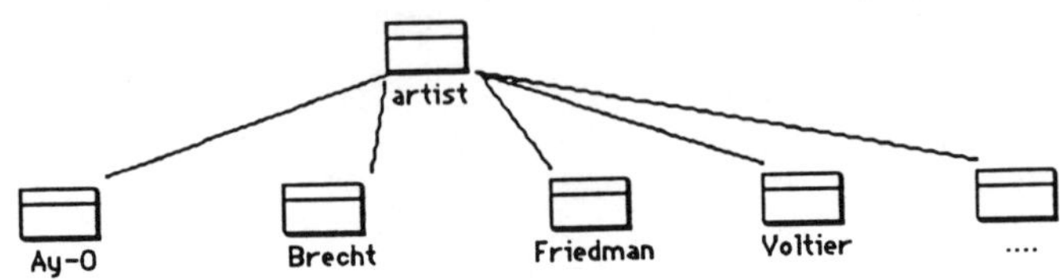

Or genre:

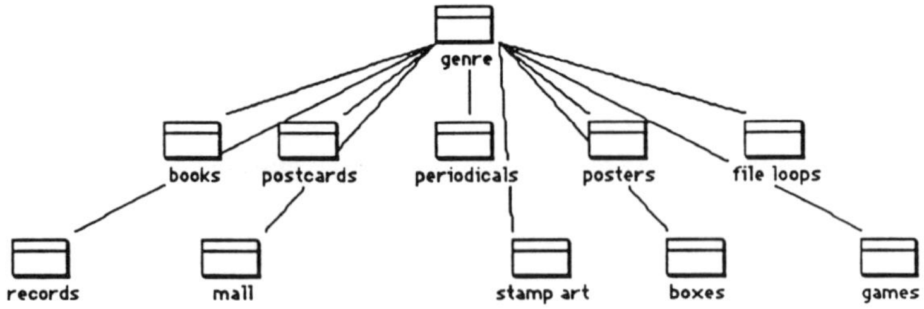

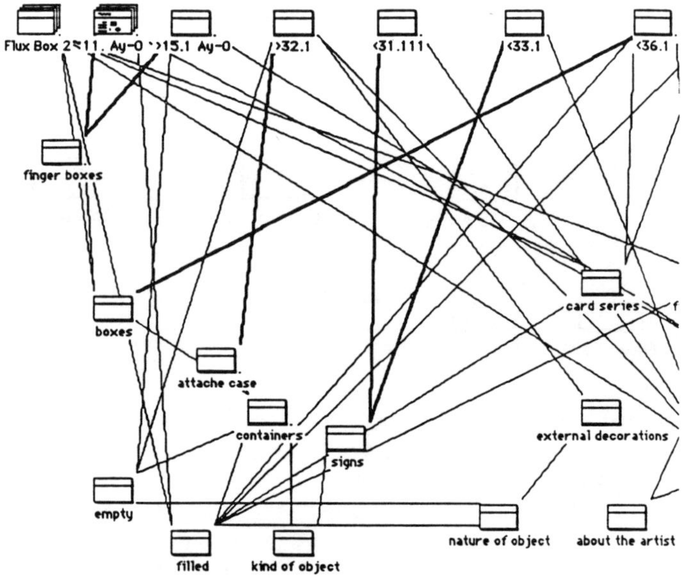

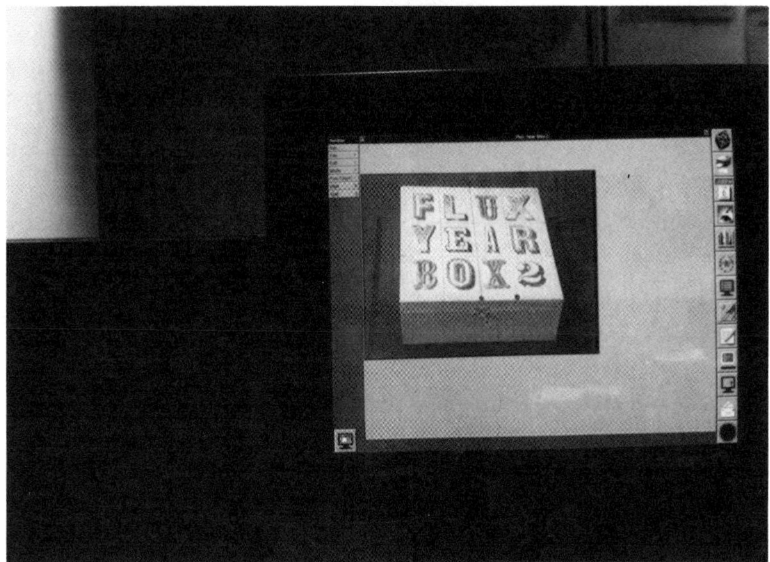

Figure 1.

In short, a rich set of cross-linked information is created. This is not astoundingly new; it is mentioned to suggest richer sets of data as well as non-textual modes of inquiry.

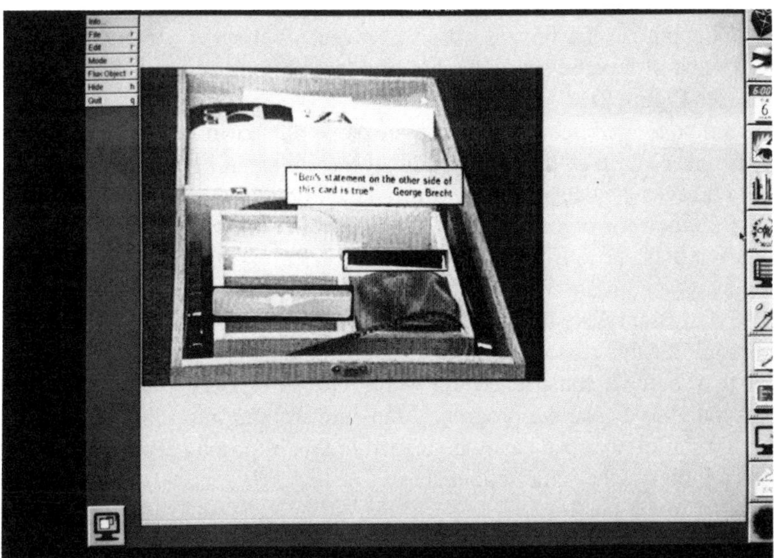

Figure 2.

Figure 3.

Description of NeXT Computer Application Prototype

Assuming the user has selected Flux Year Box 2, the closed box appears on the screen of the NeXT computer (see Figure 1).

Clicking on the box, it opens to reveal its diverse contents, a plastic box, a stack of lettered cards, the top of a tomato sculpture, a handful of film loops (see Figure 2).

Suppose we select the lettered envelope as shown in Figure 3. One by one, the user can take the monograms of the contributing artists out, placing them wherever they desire on the screen (see Figure 4).

So much for objects that are designed to be viewed as stills. But what about motion? Those film loops? Users can select a film loop (see Figure 5), and play it (see Figure 6)

Interestingly, we do not know for certain which artists contributed each film loop. For this reason, Fluxbase is constructed so that users can name the artist they believe constructed the work. This is especially important when artists themselves use the program. Many are walking repositories of insight and information that can easily be tapped in this informal network. Certainly, this is a form of electronic scholarship.

Figure 4.

Moving beyond viewing to participating, George Brecht's Games and Puzzles (see Figure 7). Opening it reveals assorted marbles, some word puzzles and so on (see Figure 8). Again, we can move them around. While presently our movements are restricted to a two dimensional surface, a greater

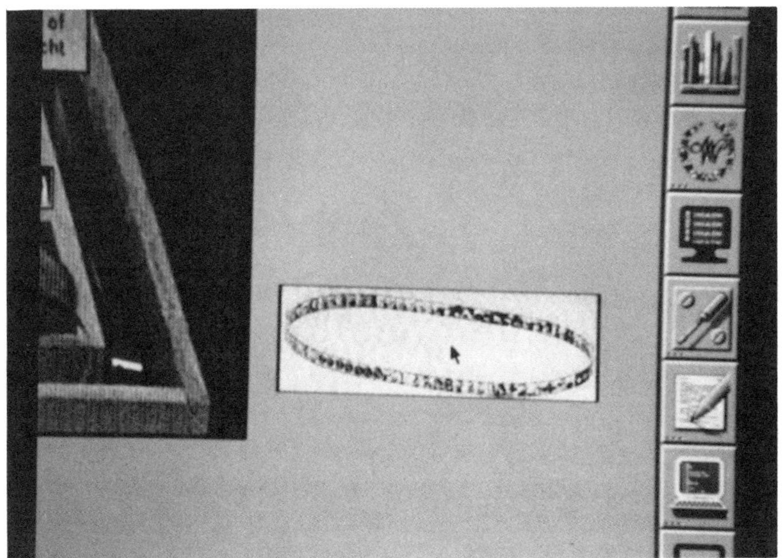

Figure 5.

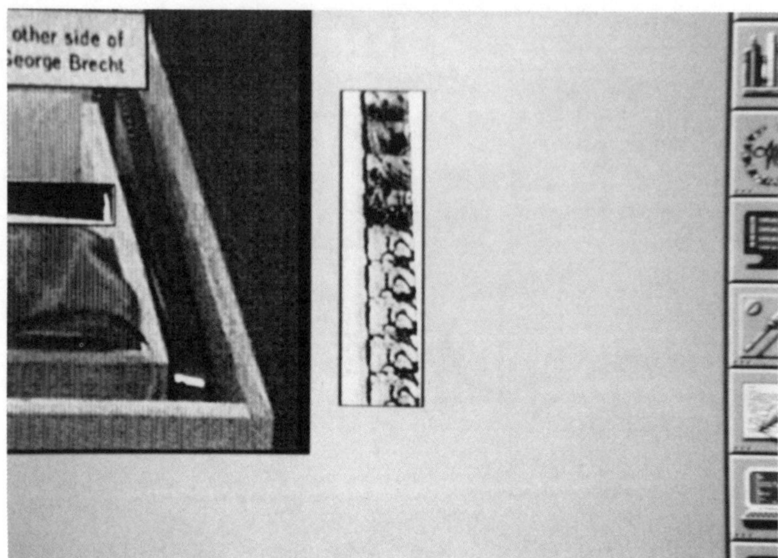

Figure 6.

three dimensional illusion will be created by increasing or decreasing the size of the digitized image as the user moves the mouse forward and backward with a depressed command key.

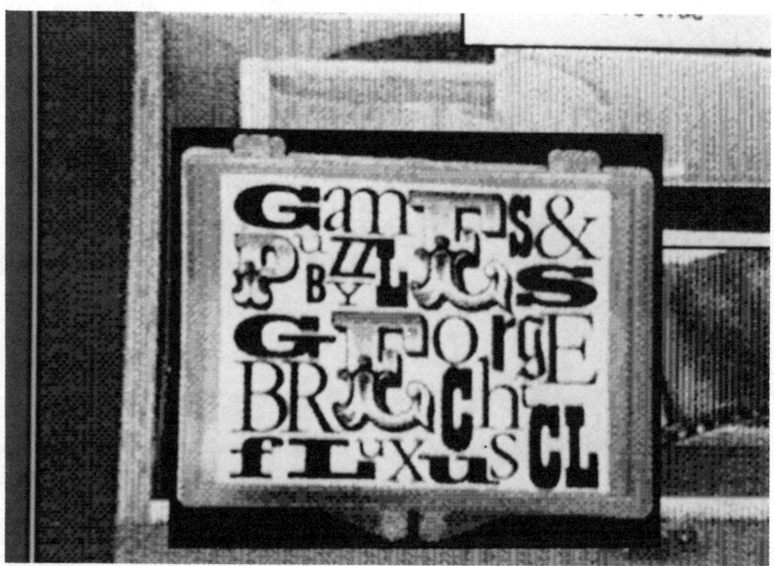

Figure 7.

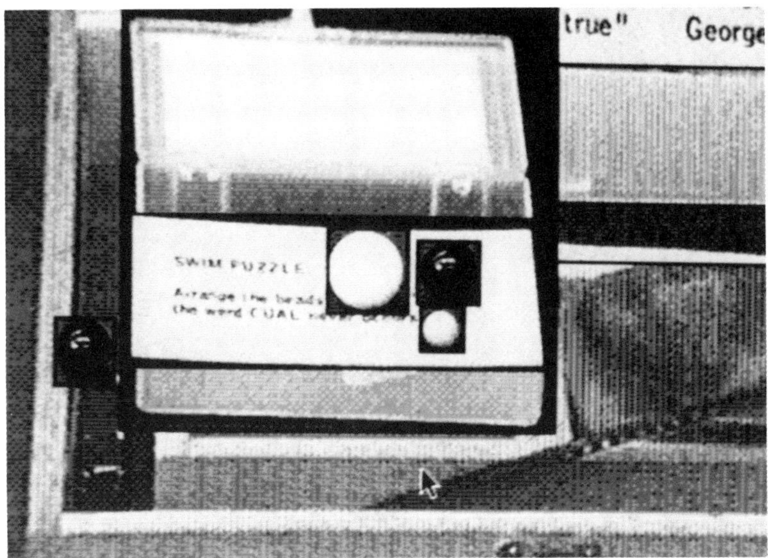

Figure 8.

Audio data will be incorporated to extend the range of information. On one side is the program (see Figure 9) and on the other side is a set of cards (see Figure 10). Just as in the real world, if you don't clean up your mess, the next person who enters the collection will be faced with a slightly untidy arrangement (see Figure 11) when cards are not put away.

In addition to selecting graphically, users can chose from a textual list as well (see Figure 12). Text is also used for the more traditional database aspects. In Figure 13, we see an annotation about Games & Puzzles peice. Another feature we plan to include is an option to view "real size" which may be smaller or larger than that presently seen on the screen.

Linking information will be displayed in a network mode; users will select a node for further information such as:

Fluxus lineage
- alternative educational systems
- Black Mountain College
- New School of Social Research

artists
- Yves Klein
- Daniel Spoerri

music
- John Cage

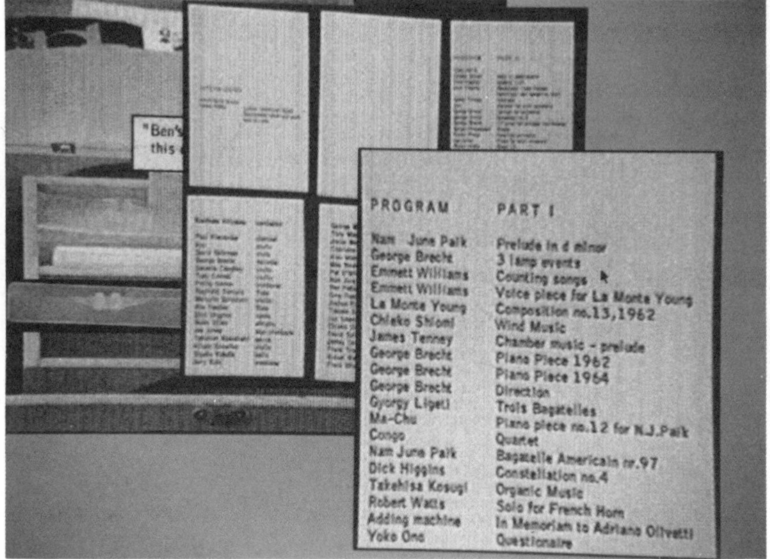

Figure 9.

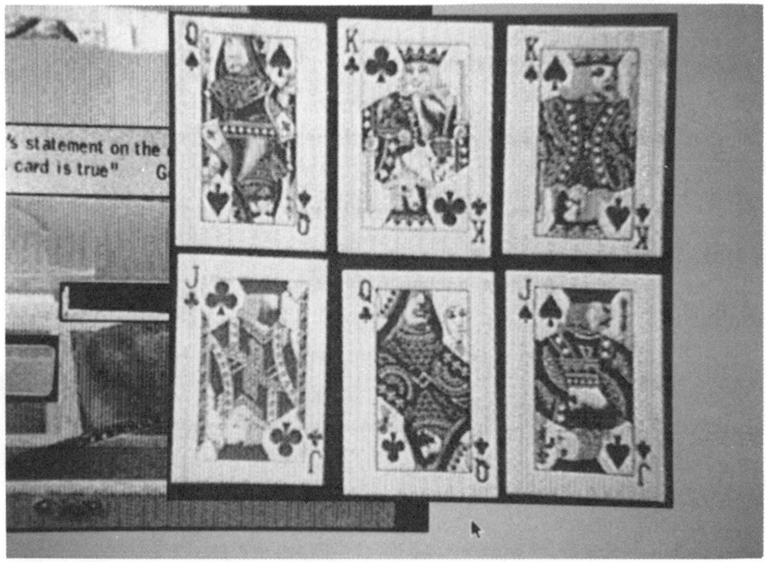

Figure 10.

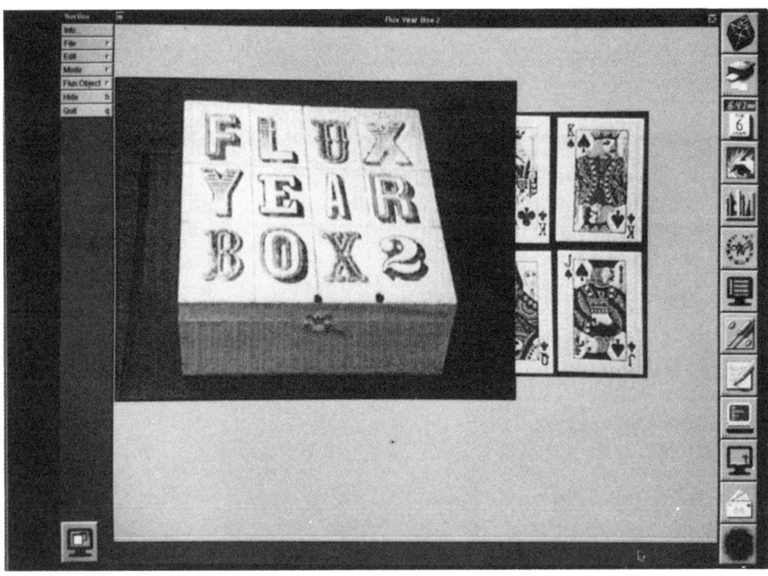

Figure 11.

- religion
- Zen Buddhism

formal characteristics of Fluxus (Higgins)

Fluxus methods of community
- mail
- mall
- press, underground
- galleries
- storefronts

Fluxus progeny
- intermedia
- correspondence art
- performance art
- book art

Selecting Hardware and Software Environment

A choice of several environments was available for developing Fluxbase: the Macintosh II, the NeXT Computer, and the IBM PS/2. At the time this project began, the most capable IBM system we had available to us was a PS/2 Model

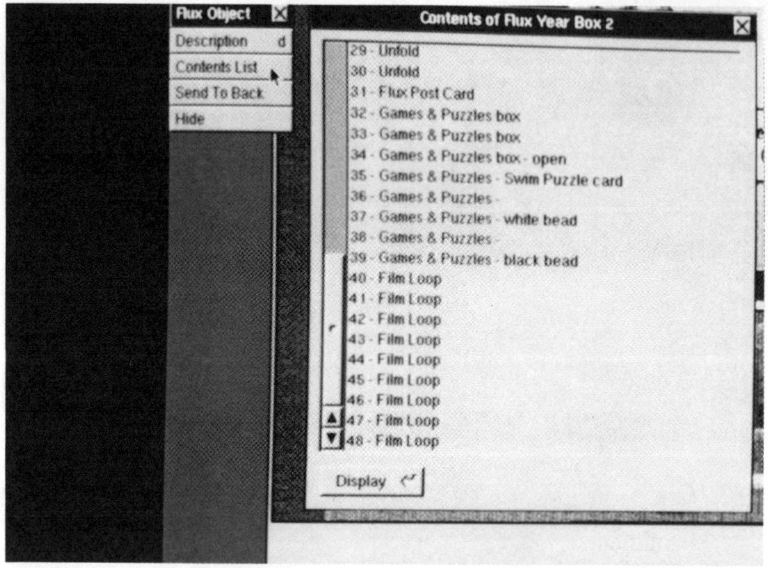

Figure 12.

30 with an EGA monitor. This platform was not robust enough to deliver the high-quality graphical display, nor was it fast enough to support the near real time manipulation necessary. The choice was narrowed to the NeXT computer and the Macintosh. The NeXT computer was a new arrival and our programming efforts had been devoted mainly to learning and evaluation. We were interested in gaining experience with the NeXT environment on a larger project, but needed to be sure that there were no overriding advantages favoring the Macintosh. We were also limited to using the resources available at the time, since there was no budget for acquiring additional hardware or software.

Hardware Considerations

A high-quality graphics display is obviously required to provide a realistic representation of a visual art object. Although the Macintosh II currently has superior color capabilities, we judged the NeXT's greyscale display adequate

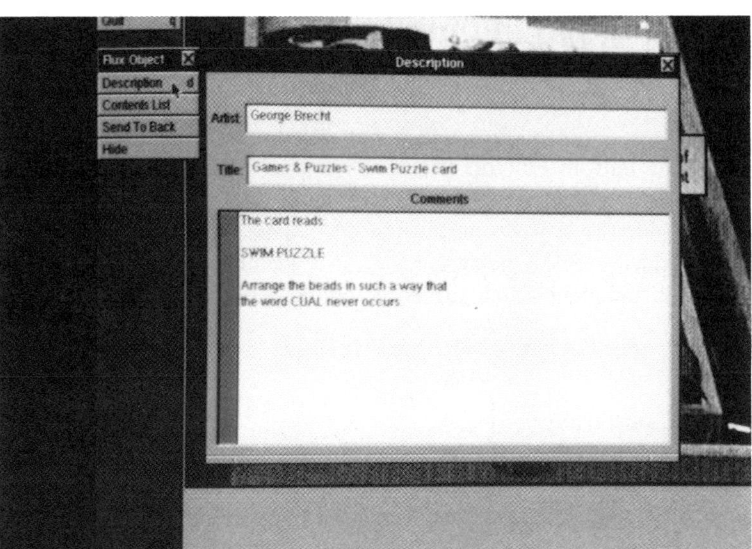

Figure 13.

for this application because the Flux Year Box 2 uses predominantly black-and-white tones. Also, the NeXT computer's standard screen provided a larger area to present and manipulate the contents of the box.

Since we planned to store a combination of color images, text, and possibly sound files, disk storage requirements were a concern. NeXT rewritable optical disks stores 256 megabytes, which is sufficient for our prototype. Optical drives for the Macintosh are still expensive, or at least beyond our budget, so it would have been necessary to use the Mac's internal 80 megabyte hard disk drive. Space here was insufficient on the Macintosh since we use this computer for a number of other ongoing projects.

Sounds requires tools for recording and playback. While the NeXT computer can record and playback CD quality sound, without external hardware for better analog-to-digital (A/D) conversion, it can only record telephone quality sound. The Macintosh has no standard hardware for A/D conversion, but we have a third party device, the Farallon MacRecorder, which allows good recordings at a reasonable cost. Although we did not incorporate audio in the initial prototype, we are including it in the expanded program. The 22 KHz sampling rate of the MacRecorder is sufficient for our needs, so we will probably record audio passages on the Mac, communicate the files to the NeXT, and convert them to a NeXT sound file.

Given that objects are housed in collections at museums across the country, and that the physical movement of objects (such as mail art) was important to the Fluxus community in particular, we wanted a future version of the program to be able to communicate with like programs at other locations. This will require potentially quite sophisticated networking capabilities. The NeXT has a built-in Ethernet port which supports much faster communications than the Macintosh's LocalTalk system. Certainly an Ethernet board could be added to the Macintosh. Indeed, practically all types of hardware could be added to make the systems virtually identical. Ultimately, it was the software environment which influenced our decision and it is to that issue we now turn.

Software Considerations

In Figure 4, we see a representative view of the box with its contents strewn around the display. Each of the "monogram cards" in the picture can be dragged around the screen, or put back in the packet from which they came. The desire to treat the computer representations of the art objects in Flux Year Box 2 as separate entities with similar behavior lends itself naturally to implementation with object-oriented methodologies; so does the construction of a graphic user interface. Therefore, our search was focused for software development tools that supported the object-oriented paradigm. On the Macintosh, was Object Pascal, HyperCard, and SuperCard. The only practical option on the NeXT computer was programming in Objective-C, using the "objects" provided in the "AppKit". This was not as limiting as it might sound, since the AppKit provides a great deal of functionality, and support for object-oriented programming techniques is fundamental to the development tools.

HyperCard is probably the most familiar of the Macintosh tools. Its cards, buttons, and message hierarchy support a limited form of object-oriented development. We immediately ruled it out, however, because it did not support color, only one card can be open at a time, and it could not treat graphic objects as separate, programmable entities. SuperCard was more promising; it had those features which HyperCard lacked, and a more powerful programming language to match.

We considered the need for additional flexibility available from a language such as Pascal or C, especially in the areas of networking and managing the manipulation of objects in window area. We did not have access to MacApp, Apple's object-oriented environment for Pascal (and now C++), so the NeXT computer was chosen.

The NeXT computer provides a rich set of software tools to support object-oriented development. Central to the system is the AppKit, a class library which provides most of the typical objects which are used to build an application with a graphic user interface, such as windows, buttons, and menus. Another class, the Bitmap, simplified using digitized images in the program. For future development, we would expect to use the Sound class for storing and playing sounds and the Speaker/Listener which allows communication between applications on local or remote systems. We also anticipate that color will be more important as we expand the kinds of art objects in the program. NeXT has promised that color video hardware will be available for the computer. Since we have used the AppKit objects and Display PostScript in the implementation; few or no program changes should be necessary to use color.

Although we chose to implement Fluxbase on the NeXT computer, we still used a Macintosh II equipped with a frame capture board to digitize the images and crop them to the desired size. We consider the prototype effort a success and hope to continue development in the NeXT environment. Still, new compilers, class libraries, and integrated environments appear regularly on all platforms and will continue to complicate decisions in the future.

Summary

The Fluxbase prototype has been demonstrated innumerable times over the past six months and has received one of two reactions. Either users say nothing and look at us as if to say “Now why would you want to do that?”. Or they smile, a big, slow, wide smile, and nod their heads up and down while saying “Now that is what a computer’s for!” To paraphrase a familiar expression, some people see the computer as it is and some people see the computer for what it can be. As users are provided with more widespread and naturalistic access to works of art — indeed to objects of interest in any field — their knowledge of, understanding about, and sheer pleasure in that field is increased and enhanced immeasurably.

References

A.A. Bronson, designer, *Evidence of the Avant Garde since 1957...*, Toronto, Canada: Art Metropole, 1984.

Frank, Peter, “Fluxus in New York”, *lightworks*, Number 11/12, Fall, 1979, pp. 29-36.

Hogan, M., “Processing Manual for Incoming Materials to Franklin Furnace Archive” (draft), Franklin Furnace Archive, Inc., New York, N.Y., 1988.

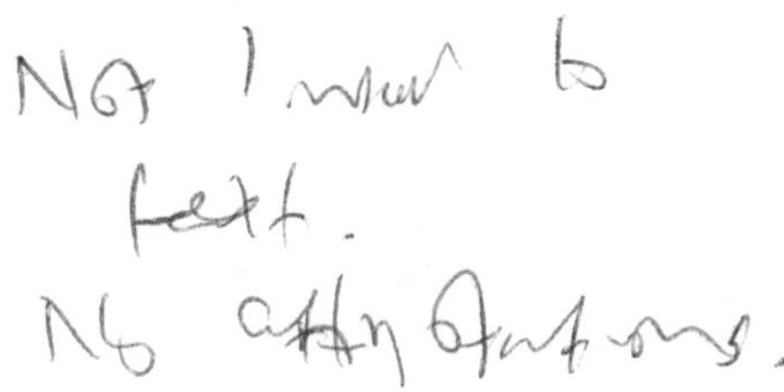

Appendix A: Recommended Readings

Alpert, M. "500,000 Pages on One Erasable Disk." *Fortune* (January 2, 1989).

Apiki, S. and Eglowstein, H. "The Optical Option." *Byte Magazine* (October, 1989): 160-174.

Araki, S., A. Asauama, and H. Kobayashi. "Magneto-Optical Writing System With the Pulse Magnetic Field." *IEEE Translation Journal on Magnetics in Japan* (1985): 691.

Asano, S. *et al.* "Magneto-Optical Recording Media With New Protective Films." In *IEEE Transactions on Magnetics*, (1987), pp. 2620-2622.

Bainbridge, R. C. "The Role of Standards in the Emerging Optical Digital Data Disk Storage Systems Market." In *Proceedings of the Society of Photo-Optical Instrumentation Engineers*, Bellingham, WA: (SPIE, 1984) 27-28.

Balafas, D.M. "Attaching Removable-Media Drives Via the File System." *Systems Integration* (November 1989): 23-24.

Balma, P. "Impact of Erasable Optical Disks on Write-Once." In *Conference Proceedings of Optical Information Systems '88*, Judith Paris Roth, 49-50. Westport, CT: Meckler Publishing , 1988.

Barton, R. *et al.* "New Phase-Change Material For Optical Recording With Short Erase Time." *Applied Physics*, 48 no 19 (1986): 1255-57.

Bate, G. "Materials Challenges in Metallic, Reversible, Optical Recording Media: A Review." In *IEEE Transactions on Magnetics, IEEE*, (1987): 151-161.

Bell, A. "Erasable Self-Biasing Thermal Magneto-Optic Medium." European Patent #86111465.0 (1986).

Bell, A. "Materials For High-Density Optical Data Storage." M. Weber (ed) *CRC Handbook of Laser Science and Technology, Volume I*. Boca Raton, FL: CRC Press, 1986.

Berg, B. A. and Roth, J.P. *Software for Optical Storage*. Westport, CT: Meckler Publishing, 1989.

Berra, P.B., and Troullinos, N.B. "Optical Techniques and Data/Knowledge Base Machines." *IEEE Computer* 20, no. 10 (October 1987): 59-70.

Berry, D. "How a Computer Media Manufacturer Approaches Erasable Optical Media Development." In *Conference Proceedings of Optical Information Systems '88*, Judith Paris Roth, 42-43. Westport, CT: Meckler Publishing, 1988.

Beshore, E. "Optotech Systems Architecture (OSA): A File System Architecture for Removable Optical Media", pp 161-167. IN: Berg, B. A. and Roth, J.P. *Software for Optical Storage*. Westport, CT: Meckler Publishing, 1989.

Birecki, H. *et al.* "Magneto-Optic Quadrilayer Reliability and Performance." In *Proceedings of the Society of Photo-Optical Instrumentation Engineers*, 19-24, 1985.

Bloomberg, D. and G. Connell. "Magnetooptical Recording." C. Mee and E. Daniel (eds.) *Magnetic Recording, Volume III*. New York: McGraw-Hill, 1988.

Boggs, R. L. "Road to Optical Digital Disk Systems: The Cautious But Optimistic User Will Lead the Way." *Journal of Information and Image Management* 19 (1986): 10-13.

Bonnebat, C. "Information Storage Technologies — Some Recent Trends and Current Prospects Analyzed From the Media Manufacturers Standpoint." *IEEE Transactions on Magnetics*, MAG-23 (1987): 9-15.

Bouwhuis, G., J. Braat, A. Huijse, J. Pasman, G. Van Rosmalen, and K. Schouhamer-Immink. *Principles of Optical Disc Systems.* Accord, MA: Adam Hilger, Ltd., 1985.

Bracker, W. E. "Optical Data Storage: Theory, Hardware, Software and Applications." In *Proceedings of the National Computer Graphics Association Graphics 87*, 75-90. Fairfax, VA: National Computer Graphics Association, 1987.

Bradley, A.C. *Optical Storage for Computers: Technical and Applications*. Ellis Horwood Books in Information Technology. New York, NY: John Wiley & Sons, 1989.

Burke, J. J. and Ryan, B. "Gigabytes Online." *Byte Magazine* (October, 1989): 259-264.

Burns, L. and E. Keizer. "Magnetic Recording System." U. S. Patent #2,915,594 (1959).

Campbell, D.K. "Drive Issues for High Performance Magneto-optic Recording." In *Topical Meeting on Optical Data Storage — Summaries of Papers*, 10:2-5. New York, NY: IEEE, 1987.

Campbell, D.K., Towner, D.K. "Magneto-Optic Polarization Readout Model." In *Topical Meeting on Optical Data Storage, A Digest of Technical Papers*. Washington, D. C.: Optical Society of America, 1986, 4 pp.

Canon USA, Inc. *Introduction to Magneto-Optic Technology: what is Magneto-Optic Storage?* Lake Success, NY: Canon USA, Inc., 1989.

Chandran, C. "Developing Erasable Optical Devices for the PC Environment." In *Conference Proceedings of Optical Information Systems '88*, Judith Paris Roth, 106-111. Westport, CT: Meckler Publishing, 1988.

Chen, D., J. Ready, and G.E. Bernal. "MnBi Thin Films: Physical Properties and Memory Applications." *Journal of Applied Physics* 39 (1968): 3916.

Choudhari, P., J. Cuomo, R. Gambino, and T. McGuire. "Beam Addressable Film Using Amorphous Magnetic Material." U.S. Patent #3,949,387 (1976).

Cinnamon, B. *Optical Disk Document Storage and Retrieval Systems.* Silver Spring, MD: Association for Information and Image Management, 1988.

Connell, G.A.N. "Magneto-Optics and Amorphous Metals: An Optical Storage Revolution." *Journal of Magnetism and Magnetic Materials*, 54, no 333 (1986): 1561-66.

Cook, E.A. "Rewritable Disks at Work in Remote Sensing/GIS." *Advanced Imaging* (September 1989): 68,71.

Costlow, T. "Erasables to Lead Op[tical] Drives Surge." *Electronic Engineering Times* (April 10, 1989).

Daly, J. "Erasable Optical Disks Step Closer to Forefront." *Computerworld* (April 10, 1989): 25, 34.

Davies, D.H. "Status of Optical Media." In *Digest of Papers: COMPCON Spring 88, Thirty-third IEEE Computer Society International Conference.* Washington, D. C.: IEEE Computer Society Press; 1988. 141-44.

Deeter, M.N., and Sarid, D. "Effects of Incident Angle on Readout in Magneto-Optic Storage Media." *Applied Optics*, 27 no 4 (1988): 713-716.

DeHaan, M. "Optical Technology: What's Mature and What's on the Horizon." *ESD: The Electronic System Design Magazine*. 17, no.9 (1987): 41-49.

Doherty, R. "Pinnacle to Ship Jukebox." *Macintosh News* (August 21, 1989): 48.

"Erasable Optical Drives: Here Real Soon." *ByteWeek* (January 1989): 2.

Evans, R. "Reaping the Full Benefits of End-User Computing."*Computerworld* (August 21, 1989): 67-71.

Freedman, J. B. "The Institute for Computer Science and Technology at the National Bureau of Standards (NBS/ICST) Optical Digital Data Disk Standardization Activities." In *Proceedings of the Society of Photo-Optical Instrumentation Engineers*, 77-79. Bellingham, WA: SPIE, 1987.

Freese, R. P. *et al.* "An Environmentally Stable, High Performance, High Data Rate Magneto-Optic Media." In *Proceedings of the Society of Photo-Optical Instrumentation Engineers*, 529 (1985): 6-11.

Freese, R. P. "Optical Disks Become Erasable." *IEEE Spectrum* 25, no. 2 (1988): 41-45.

Freese, R. P., M. DeHaan, and A. A. Jamberdino, eds. *Optical Mass Data Storage: Proceedings of the SPIE (The International Society for Optical Engineering) Meeting*. Bellingham, WA: SPIE, 1986.

Funkenbusch, A.W. *et al.* "Magneto-Optics Technology for Mass Storage Systems." In *Digest of Papers, Eighth IEEE Symposium on Mass Storage Systems: Emerging Solutions for Data- Intensive Applications*, K. Friedman, 101-106. Washington, D. C.: IEEE Computer Society Press, 1987.

Galic, G. "Alternative Approaches to Conventional Erasable Optical Disk Substrate Manufacturing." In *Conference Proceedings of Optical Information Systems '88*, Judith Paris Roth, 53-57. Westport, CT: Meckler Publishing, 1988.

Gardner, R. H, V. W. Halling, T. A. Rinehart, A. W. Funkenbusch, M. A. Khan, D. W. Siitari, and R. P. Freese. "Status of M/O Erasable Media Production." In *Proceedings of the Topical Meeting on Optical Data Storage*, 120-122. New York, NY: IEEE, 1987.

Gardner, R. N., S. Webster, S, M. A. Khan, T. A., Rinehart, and A. W. Funkenbusch. "M/O: Its Emergence as the Dominant Erasable Technology." In *Optical Mass Data Storage: Proceedings of the SPIE (The International Society for Optical Engineering) Meeting*, edited by R. P. Freese, *et al.*, 48-55. Bellingham, WA: SPIE, 1986.

Gardner, R.N., T.A. Rinehart, Johnson, L.H., Freese, R.P., and Lund, R.A. "Characteristics of a New High C/N Magneto-Optic Media." In *Optical Storage Media: Proceedings of the SPIE (The International Society for Optical Engineering) Meeting*, 242-248. Bellingham, WA: SPIE, 1983.

Garfinkel, S.L. "Optical Drives for MS-DOS." *MIPS* (August 1989): 74-83.

Gaskin, R.R. "Paper, Magnets, and Light." *BYTE Magazine* (November 1989): 391-399.

Gravesteijn, D.J. "Materials Developments for Write-Once and Erasable Phase-Change Optical Recording." *Applied Optics*, 27 no 4 (1988): 736-738.

Gunn, Keith. "File Structure Standards." *Optical Memory News*, 63 (1988): 6-7.

Gupta, M. and F. Strome. "Erasable Laser Recording in an Organic Dye-Binder Optical Disc Medium." *Journal of Applied Physics*. 60 (1986): 2932.

Hallam, K. "Current Status of Optical Media Standards", pp 153-156. Berg, B. A. and Roth, J.P. *Software for Optical Storage*. Westport, CT: Meckler Publishing, 1989.

Hartman, J.S., Braat, J., Jacobe, B. "Erasable Magneto-Optical Recording Media." *IEEE Transactions on Magnetics*, 1013-1018, 1984.

Hecht, J. "Optical Memories Vie for Data Storage." *High Technology Business* (August 1987).

Hoaglund, A. S. "Information Storage Technology: A Look at the Future." *Computer* (July, 1985).

Imamura, N. "Magneto-Optical Disk Memory." *Information Processing Society of Japan*, 26 no 1 (1985): 25-32.

Introduction to Magneto-Optic Technology: What is Magneto-Optic Storage? Published by Canon USA, Inc. 1989.

Isailovic, J. *Videodisc and Optical Memory Systems*. Englewood Cliffs, NJ: Prentice-Hall, Inc., 1985.

Itoh, K.I., *et al.* " Analog Full-Motion Video Recording on Magneto-Optical Disk." *Sharp Technical Journal* (Japan), 39 (1988): 49-53.

Iwanaga, T. *et al.* "Magneto-Optic Recording Readout Performance Improvement." *Applied Optics*, 27 no 4 (1988): 717-22.

Jipson, V. B. "Erasable Optical Recording Technologies." In *Topical Meeting on Optical Data Storage — Summaries of Papers*, 146. New York, NY: IEEE, 1987.

Kalstrom, D. *Compatibility is the Key to Success for New Computer Technologies*. Plasmon Data Systems, Inc., 1988.

Kalstrom, D. "Hard Disk Vs. Erasable Optical Storage." *Computer Systems News*, May 1, 1989: 17.

Kikuchi, N. *et al.* "Erasable CD-compatible magneto-optical disk recorder." *Journal of the Audio Engineering Society*, 32 (1984): 1011.

Kobayashi, M. *et al.* "Corrosion Resistance of Magneto-Optical Recording Media." *Journal of Magnetics* Japan (IEEE Translation), 2 (1987): 404-405.

Kuttner, P. "Optics for Data Storage: Optical Disk Technology." In *Laser Beam Scanning: Opto-Mechanical Decisions, Systems*, edited by G. F. Marshall, 303-409. New York, NY: Marcel Dekker, Inc., 1985.

Kume, M., Ito, K., Kano, G. "Semiconductor Lasers for WORM, Erasable and Rewritable Memory Disks." *Journal of Electronic Engineering*, 24 no 248 (1987): 44-47.

Kwok, C. "Implementing WORM and Erasable Optical Storage in the OS/2 Environment." In *Software for Optical Storage*. Westport, CT: Meckler Publishing, 1989.

Lang, L. "Erasable Drives Face Hurdles." *Computer Systems News* (March 5, 1990): 54-55.

Lange, G. R. "Practical Specifications for Characterizing Write/Read Performance of Optical Disk Media." In *Topical Meeting on Optical Data Storage — Summaries of Papers*, 54-57. New York, NY: IEEE, 1987.

Lapedus, M. "HP Sees Broad Market for Erasable Drive." *Electronic News*, (April 17, 1989): 24.

Lee, K. "Magnetic Thin Films for Optical Storage." *Journal of Vacuum Science and Technology* 10 (1973): 631.

Lenth, W., R. Macfarlane, W. Moerner, F. Schellenberg, R. Shelby, and G. Bjorklund. "High-Density Frequency-Domain Optical Recording." *SPIE Proceedings* 695 (1986): 216.

Lewicki, G. and J. Guisinger. "Thermomagnetic Recording and Magneto-Optic Playback System." U. S. Patent #3,626,114 (1971).

Lindmayer, J. "A New Erasable Optical Memory." *Solid State Technology* (August 1988).

Little, J.P. "PDO and Erasable Technology. In *Conference Proceedings of Optical Information Systems '88*, Judith Paris Roth, 36-41. Westport, CT: Meckler Publishing, 1988.

Lynch, C. A. "Optical Storage Media, Standards, and Technology Life Cycle Management." *Records Management Quarterly* 20, no. 1 (1986): 44-54.

Magel, M. "Write-Once and Erasable Alternatives." *AV Video*, (November 1988): 36-38,4 7.

Marchant, A.B. *Optical Recording: A Technical Overview*. Reading, MA: Addison-Wesley Publishing Company, 1990.

Mayer, L. "Curie-Point Writing on Magnetic Films." *Journal of Applied Physics* 29 (1958): 1003.

McCready, S. "CD-WORM and Erasable Versus WORM: The Future Battle." In *Conference Proceedings of Optical Information Systems '88*. Judith Paris Roth, 125-127. Westport, CT: Meckler Publishing, 1988.

Meng, B. "Systems Architecture: Optical Disks Slip in Compatibility." *Digital Design* 16, no. 1 (1986): 28-37.

Meyer, F. "Erasable Optical: No Hard Disk Replacement." *Computer Technology Review* (May 1, 1989): 24.

Meyer, F. "Erasable Optical No Mark Threat." *Computer Technology Review* March, 1989: 26.

Minemura, H., Tsuboi, N., Sato, Y. "Erasable Characteristics of Optical Disks Using Induction Heating." *Transactions of the Institute of Electronic Information Communication Engineers*. 3 (1988): 486-91.

Minemura, T., H. Andoh, and Y. Maeda. "Reversible Color Changes in Sputter-Deposited Ag-Zn Alloy Films." *Journal of Applied Physics* 63 (1988): 4632.

Mitsuhashi, Y. "Standardization Activities for Optical Data Disk in Japan." In *Proceedings of the Society of Photo-Optical Instrumentation Engineers*, 71-73. Bellingham, WA: SPIE, 1984.

Moerner, W., R. Macfarlane, and W. Lenth. "Frequency Domain Optical Storage: The Importance of Photon-Gated Materials." *Topical Meeting on Optical Data Storage*. 10 (1987): 151.

Nagato, K., A. Kawamoto, T. Sato, and Y. Yorozu. "Compositional Dependence of Recording Noise in Amorphous Rare-Earth - Transition-Metal Magneto-Optical Discs." *Journal of Applied Physics* 63 (1988): 3856.

"The NeXT Debut: The Computing Landscape Changes." *Seybold Report on Desktop Publishing*. (Media, PA: Seybold Publicaitons, Inc.) October 12, 1988.

Nishioka, Y. "Rewritable Magneto-Optical Disk Drive Unit." *Journal of Electronic Engineering* (Japan), 24 no 249 (1987): 4-77.

Nugent, W. R. "Error Detection and Correction Systems for Optical Disks: Issues of Media Defect Distribution, Defect Growth, Error Management and Disk Longevity." In *Optical Mass Data Storage: Proceedings of the SPIE (The International Society for Optical En-*

gineering), edited by R. P. Freese, *et al.*, 10-15. Bellingham, WA: SPIE, 1986.

Ohr, S. "Magneto-Optics Combines Erasability and High-Density Storage." *Electronic Design*, 33 no 16 (1985): 93-98,100.

Office Productivity Using Image Storage and Retrieval Systems. Saratoga, CA: Electronic Trend Publications, 1988. $295.

Ojima, M., T. Nakao, H. Sukeda, N. Ohta, H. Yasuoka, T. Nishida, and M. Terao. "High-Speed Overwritable Optical Disc." *SPIE Proceedings* 899 (1988): 154.

Ojima, M. *et al.* "Compact Magneto-Optical Disk for Coded Data Storage." *Applied Optics*, 25 (1986): 483-89.

Okada, M. *et a*l. "High C/N Magneto-Optical Disks Using Plastic Substrates for Video Image Applications." *IEEE Transactions on Magnetics*, 23 no 5 (1987): 2699-2701.

The Optical Storage Primer. San Diego, CA: Hewlett-Packard, 1989.

Optical Technology's Impact on Paper, Microform, Magnetic and Tape Storage: A Technology Impact Report Describing the Growth Opportunities and Applications for CD-ROM, CD Interface Disks, WORM, and Erasable Optical Drives. Saratoga, CA: Electronic Trend Publications, 1988. $1,250.

Ota, K. "Sharp Originates Four-Layer Film Rewritable Magneto-Optical Disk." *Journal of Electronic Engineering* (Japan), 24 no 248 (1987):88-90.

Ovshinsky, S. "Method and Apparatus for Storing and Retrieving Information." U.S. Patent #3,530,441 (1970).

"PDO To Produce Erasable Optical Discs." *MedicalDisc Reporter* (November/December 1988): 2.

Radoff, D. "New Choices in Storage." *Unix World* (April, 1989): 69-72.

Raval, H. "CCTA and MoD Bureau West Rewritable Optical Disk Project." *Information Media and Technology* 22, no 4 (1989): 170-173.

Reilly, L. "Tiny Quantex Rides on Potential of Big Ideas, The Biggest Being Erasable Optical Disks." *New Technology Week* Vol 2, no 49 (December 12, 1988).

Reinhardt, A. "Discus Rewritable: The Latest in Storage Technology." *Byte Magazine* (April, 1989): 102, 104.

"Rewritable Optical Storage Enhances LANs." *LAN Times* (July 1, 1989): 36.

"Rewritable Opticals Need Polishing." *MacWeek* (July 1, 1989): 62.

Rimbart, A. " Wiping the Slate Clean With Erasable Disks." *Electronic Times* 350 (1986): 34-35.

Rothchild, E. "1990: The Year of the Rewritable Drive." *Optical Memory News* 79 (January 1990): 1, 9-13.

Rothchild, E. *Rewritable Optical Media and Technology Markets.* San Francisco, CA: Rothchild Consultants, 1988.

Rothchild, E. "An Eye on Optical Disks." *Datamation* (March 1, 1986).

Rugar, D. "Magneto-Optic Direct Overwrite Using a Resonant Bias Coil." *IEEE Transactions on Magnetics*, 24 no 1 (1988): 666- 669.

Sadashige, K., and Takenaga, M. "Optical Disk Technology for Permanent and Erasable Memory Applications." *Journal of the Society of Motion Picture and Television Engineers*, 94 (1985): 200-05.

Saffady, W. *Optical Disks for Data and Document Storage.* Westport, CT: Meckler Publishing, 1988.

Saffady, W. *Optical Storage Technology: A Bibliography.* Westport, CT: Meckler Publishing, 1989.

Saffady, W. *Optical Storage Technology 1987: A State-of-the-Art Review.* Westport, CT: Meckler Publishing, 1987.

Saffady, W. *Optical Storage Technology 1988: A State-of-the-Art Review.* Westport, CT: Meckler Publishing, 1988.

Sander, I., and S. Slovenkai. "Magneto-Optical Recording with a Compact Optical Head." In *Proceedings of the Society of Photo-Optical Instrumentation Engineers (SPIE): Third International Conference on Optical Mass Data Storage*, 182-185. Bellingham, WA: SPIE, 1985.

Saito, J., M. Sato, H. Matsumoto, and H. akasaka. "Direct Overwrite by Light Power Modulation on Magneto-Optical Mutilayered Media." *International Symposium on Optical Memory 1987, Technical Digest*, 9.

Sato, M. *et al.* "Reliability of Magneto-Optical Memory Disks." *Journal of Magnetics Japan* (IEEE Translation) 2 (1987): 395-96.

Satoh, H. *et al.* "Magneto-Optical Erasable Disc Drive." In *Video, Audio, and Data Recording - Proceedings of the Seventh International Conference*. London: IERE, 79 (1988): 15-20.

Savage, J.A. "Optical Disks Breaking Ground." *Computerworld* (August 14, 1989): 21, 28.

Schein, A. "Optical Storage and OCR - Key Components of Automated Information Management Systems." *Optical Information Systems* 9, no. 1 (1989): 9-15.

Scholte, P.M.L.O., Gravesteijn, D.J.. "New Materials for Reversible Optical Storage Applications." In *Video, Audio, and Data Recording - Proceedings of the Seventh International Conference*. London: IERE, 79 (1988): 11-14.

Schroeder, C. "Information Standards and Optical Disk Systems." *Inform* 1, no.2 (1987): 12-13.

Seiter, C. "Hard Disk Alternatives." *Macworld* (July 1989): 116-122.

Seiter, C. "Erasable Opticals: New Light on Data." *Macworld: The Macintosh Magazine* (March 1990): 152-159.

Shieh, J. and M. Kryder. "Magneto-optic Recording Materials with Direct Overwrite Capability." *Applied Physics Letters* 49 (1986): 473.

Simpson, D. "Erasable Optical Disks: When, What, Why?" *Mini- Micro Systems* 20, no. 12 (December 1987): 15-18.

Simpson, D. "Write-Once, Read-Many, Why Wait?" *Mini-Micro Systems* 21, no. 12 (December 1988): 76-83.

Soat, J. and McClatchy, W. "A Different Orientation." *Information Week* (February 12, 1990): 46-47.

"Steve Jobs on PostScript, Quickdraw, and the NeXT Computer." *Publish!* (October, 1989): 46-49.

Taira, K. *et al.* "Magneto-Optic Erasable Disc Memory with Two Optical Heads." In *Topical Meeting on Optical Data Storage, A Digest of Technical Papers.* Washington, D. C.: Optical Society of America, 1985.

Takahashi, T., Gardner, R., Funkenbusch, A.W., Rinehard, T.A., and Siitari, D. "Performance of Magneto-Optic Media on Plastic Substrates." (MAG-86-88) 1986. Available from 3M Optical Recording Products.

Takayama, S., T. Niihara, K. Kaneko, Y. Sugita, and M. Ojima. "Magnetic and Magneto-Optical Properties of Tb-Fe-Co Amorphous Films." *Journal of Applied Physics* 61 (1987): 2610.

Takenaga, M., N. Yamada, S. Ohara, K. Nishiuchi, M. Nagashima, T. Kashihara, S. Nakarmura, and T. Yamashita. "New Optical Erasable Medium Using Tellurium Suboxide Thin Film." *SPIE Proceedings* 420 (1983): 173.

Tanaka, K., Watanbe, I., Sugahara, H. "The Technical Trends in Optical Disk Storage." *Information Processing Society of Japan* 28, no. 8 (1987): 1075-83.

Tevanian, Jr., Avadis and Smith, B. "Mach: The Model for Future UNIX." *BYTE Magazine* (November 1989): 411-416.

Thomas, G.E. "Future Trends in Optical Recording." *Philips Technical Review* (Netherlands), 44 no 2 (1988): 51-57.

Thompson, T. and Nick Baran. "The NeXT Computer." *Byte Magazine* 13, no. 12 (November 1988): 158-175.

Torazawa, K. etal. "Erasable Digital Audio Disc System." In *Topical Meeting on Optical Data Storage, A Digest of Technical*

Papers, Washington, D. C.: Optical Society of America, 1985.

Tsunoda, Y. "Present Status and Future Trends in Erasable Optical Memories." In *Topical Meeting on Optical Data Storage, A Digest of Technical Papers*, Washington, D. C.: Optical Society of America, 1985.

Tsunoda, Y., and Ojima, M. "Advanced Technologies For the Next Generation Optical Disks." In *Topical Meeting on Optical data Storage, A Digest of Technical Papers*, 60-63. Washington, D. C.: Optical Society of America, 1987.

Tyan, Y.S. *et al.* "Recent Advances in Phase-Change Media." In *Topical meeting on Optical Data Storage, A Digest of Technical Papers*, 44-49. Washington, D. C.: Optical Society of America, 1987.

Understanding Computers: Memory and Storage. Alexandria, VA: Time-Life Books, Inc., 1987.

van Uijen, C.M. "Reversible Optical Recording: Phase-Change Media and Magneto-Optics." *Proceedings of the Society of Photo-Optical Instrumentation Engineers*, 2-5, 1985.

Verhueven, J. A. "Standardization Activities of Optical Digital Data Technology in European Computer Manufacturers Association (ECMA)." In *Proceedings of the Society of Photo-Optical Instrumentation Engineers*, 74-76. Bellingham, WA: SPIE, 1984.

Warren, C. "Software Tools, Utilities Drive Optical Disks." *Mini-Micro Systems* 19, no. 15 (December 1986): 33-44.

Watabe, A. Yamamoto, M., Katoh, K. "High-Speed Recording Technology for Optical Disk Compatible Between Write-once and Magneto-Optical Media." *Review of the Electronics Communications Laboratory*, 36 no 2 (1988): 261-66.

Webb, D. "Erasable Optical Comes of Age." *Computer Systems News* (June 5, 1989): 33.

Webster, B. *The NeXT Book.* New York, NY: Addison-Wesley, 1989.

Webster, B. "What's NeXT?" *Macworld: The Macintosh Magazine* (January 1989).

Williams, H., R. Sherwood, F. Foster, and E. Kelly. "Magnetic Writing on Thin Films of MnBi." *Journal of Applied Physics* 28 (1957): 1181.

Wirbel, L. "NeXT Gets OS, Application Packages." *Electronic Engineering Times* (September 25, 1989): 15.

Yasuoka, H., M. Ojima, M. Terao, and T. Nishida. "Novel 1-Beam-Overwriting Method for Phase-Change Erasable Disk." *International Symposium on Optical Memory 1987, Technical Digest*, 21.

Zajaczkowski, J. "Future Standardization Development Projects Within the ANSI." In *Proceedings of the Society of Photo-Optical Instrumentation Engineers*, 68-70. Bellingham, WA: SPIE, 1984.

Zhou, Z., Chin, K., Wang, M. "Optical and Thermal Analysis of Erasable Optical Storage." In *Topical Meeting on Optical Data Storage: Summaries of Papers*, 142-144. Washington, D. C.: Optical Society of America, Technical Digest Series, 1987.

ANSI X3B11 Committee Documents for 5.25-inch Erasable Optical Disk

X3B11/88-094R3	130mm Rewritable Media, Continuous Composite-Servo (CCS).

Appendix B: Glossary of Terms and Acronyms

Whether they consist of one word or several words, the terms that follow are listed in alphabetical order, letter by letter, up to the comma in the case of inversion. Identical terms with different meanings are defined under a single heading in a series of numbered definitions.

A

ACCESS TIME: The time to get to a specified location in or on a memory device. For disk drives, quoted access times usually refer only to the positioning time for the radial actuator, neglecting servo settling and rotational latency; average access times for disk drives usually describe a radial motion of one-third of a full stroke; see latency.

ALGORITHM: Mathmematical/computational expression or formula for problem solving.

ANALOG: Continuously variable measurement or output of a physical function or quantity such as voltage, temperature, sound wave or an electrical current.

ARRAY: Arrangement of elements in a pattern such as dots on a printed page or pixels on a display monitor.

ASCII: Abbreviation for American Standard Code for Information Interchange. A convention that assigns a standard binary code to each upper- and lower-case character, numeral and typographical symbol.

ATL: Abbreviation for Automated Tape Library.

B

BACKWARDS COMPATIBLE: Sometimes "downward compatible;" said of a new product which can be used with equipment or media originally design for use with an older product. An example would be erasable medium which can be written and read by a drive that was originally produced to read and write write-once media.

BAD SECTOR: An unwritable portion of an optical disk caused by a media defect. A 'bad sector' plots these locations and prevents I/O to them.

BINARY IMAGE: Black and white image with no grey shades.

BIT-MAP/MAPPED: Pixels or image data bits are acquired, stored or mapped into computer memory, and/or displayed in the exact position as in the original document. Bitmapping is produced by raster scanning.

BLACK AND WHITE SCANNER: Detects only black or white. With additional software, a black and white scanner can perform dotting, electronic screening, or dithering to produce simulated grey-scale pixel configurations.

BLOCK: An amount of data moved or addressed as a single unit; the least amount of data to be read or written at a time. Deciding what size a block should be involves trade-offs. Error correction will use the least additional storage space when blocks are long, but storage space is wasted if a data file is smaller than a block. Typical block sizes in WORM drives are 0.5 kB to 2kB. Under DOS or OS/2 a virtual drive can reside on multiple or a single storage platter. A logical block device would be represented as a single drive letter.

BURST: In error correction, the loss of many consective bits of information, usually because of some flaw in the medium such as a scratch or dirt. The distinction is with continuous noise which corrupts data in a different way, requiring a different kind of error correction. In optical memory, most data loss is due to burst errors. The design of an error correction code depends on how often error bursts are likely to occur and how long the longest burst is likely to be.

C

CACHE: Generally temporary storage for data to which access must be very quick.

CARTRIDGE: In optical technology, an enclosure, generally of plastic, in which an optical medium is kept for protection. Some vendors captivate their media in the cartridge (this mode is called "spin in"), providing a window for the light beams; others remove the medium from the cartridge inside the drive. Also called cassette.

CAV (Constant Angular Velocity): Describes a disk which always spins at the same rotational rate, so that the time take to scan a track is the same at all radii.

CCD: Abbrebiation for Charge-Coupled Device. Solid state charge-coupled sensor detects reflect light from a scanned document and converts the light to an electrical signal for digitization.

CCITT: Abbreviation for the International Telegraph and Telephone Consultative Committee. Established compression techniques. Groups 1, 2, 3, and 4 are industrial standards for facsimile scanned information communication and data compression.

Group 1 is a bit-map raster standard for use in facsimile transmission of analog signals. Stores each pixel.

Group 2 uses the Huffman run-length code, one-dimensional means to compress raster files for use in facsimile transmission of analog signals.

Group 3 is a two-dimensional means of compressing 200 dpi raster files for use in facsimile transmission of documents.

Group 4 is the standard for digital, high-speed 200-400 dpi data transmission.

Group 3 and Group 4 are oriented towards page size documents and are being successfully adaptered by system integrators to engineering document maangement systems by partitioning large format documents into multiple page size areas. Attainable compression ratios are in the range of 10:1 for Group 3 and 20:1 for Group 4.

CLV (Constant Linear Velocity): Describes a disk which turns more slowly when outer radii are being scanned so that the relative velocity between the light spot and the track is maintained at a constant value. This keeps the linear density of data constant over the whole disk, but creates practical problems due to the non-constant time taken to scan one track and the need to speed up and slow down the disk as various radii are scanned.

CIRC (Cross-Interleaved Reed-Solomon Code):Using a sophisticated method of error detection and correction (a layered error correction code) that involves techniques of data delay and data rearrangement techniques, corrected data can be one bit error in a trillion bits. CIRC detects and corrects up to two errors in one code word and interpolates for long error bursts. The maximum complete correctably error burst length is 4,000 data bits, and the maximum worst case interpolatable burst is 12,300 data bits assuming that no random errors occur at the same time.

COMPRESSION: A technique that saves storage space by eliminating gaps, empty fields, redundancy, or unnecessary data, to shorten the length of records or blocks using CCITT standards. Provides for the transmission of fewer data bits than originally required within information loss. The receiving location implements the reverse operation to convert it to the original data.

D

DEFECT: Some irregularity in a medium which disturbs its ability to carry recorded data. Defects in an optical disk include bumps, depressions, dirt, missing sensitive material, etc. Because of the high density of optical recording, even micrometer sized defects are import.

DEFECT DENSITY: The fraction of the total active area of a medium obscured by defects.

DITHERING: Also referred to as electronic screening. Method used by some scanners to simulate intermediate shades of grey. Geometric pixel patterns of various sizes are created according to the brightness of the image area.

DOS: OS/2 Device Driver:Software modules written for DOS or OS/2 which control hardware, typically a storage device such as WORM, and isolates the higher levels of the operating system from the specific idiosyncracies of the hardware device.

DRAW (Direct-Read-After-Write): Describes the method of error checking in which data written to an optical disk during one disk rotation is read for accuracy on the subsequent rotation. Recorded data on an optical disk may be read immediately after writing (recording); no processing is required. This allows error free recording in a single pass because whenever a written sector of data contains errors it is immediately rewritten.

DRDW (Direct-Read-During-Write): Describes a method of error checking data on an optical disk in which data is written and verified during the same disk rotation. Refers to the ability to read the information during the writing (recording) process.

E

ELECTRONIC SCREENING: See Dithering.

ERROR CORRECTION CODE (ECC): A method of data recovery that allows the full recovery of a single physical block of user data which is 2,048 bytes. A code which turns a bit stream into a longer bit stream whose length comes from carefully designed redundancy. This is intended to enable the encoded bit stream to survive corruption by random noise and burst noise and still be decodable to the original bit stream without missing or wrong data. An example is CIRC, and convolutional code.

ERROR DETECTION CODE (EDC): Used in conjunction with ECC, EDC allows the detection of errors for correction.

F

FARADAY EFFECT: Certain substances, when exposed to a magnetic field, will change the polarity of light passing through them. This polarity change is called the Farady effect. Optical disks using the Faraday effect must be transmissive, rather than reflective.

FAT (File Allocation Table): A DOS or OS/2 data structure maintained by the operating system on the drive partition. Through the FAT, DOS or OS/2 finds the appropriate chain of logical sectors which comprise a file.

FILE HEADER: A data structure containing information about a file, stored in memory or on disk. Analogous to the Unix “inode”.

FILE SERIAL NUMBER: A sequence number assigned to files as they are created. Used to identify files after they have been opened.

FILE SYSTEM GENERATION NUMBER: A version number of the ODFS stored in some control records on the optical disk.

FIRMWARE: Prewritten programs stored in read-only memory (ROM) circuits. Used widely as a method of implementing commonly used software in word processing and small computer systems.

FLUSH: To write a write buffer to the optical disk.

FLYING SPOT SCANNER: Scanning mechanism is attached to the light source so that the light moves over or under the document or micro-image.

FORM FACTOR: The size and shape of a product. For example, most 5.25-inch Winchester drives have the same dimensions so that they can fit interchangeably into computer cabinets. For the same reason, 5.25-inch optical drives are expected to have the same form factor as Winchesters.

G

GB: Gigabyte. The prefix “giga” means one billion; GB refers to one gigabyte.

H

HALF-TONE: Production of a continuous-tone photograph through a contact screen which breaks up the image into various-size dots to simulate shades of grey.

HANDLING ZONE: The part of a disk that may be touched by a handling mechanism, e.g., in a jukebox.

HIGH WATER MARK: The sector number of the last-written sector on the optical disk, not counting Unmount Record sectors.

I

IGES: Initial Graphics Exchange Specification which defines a standard for mat used for transferring CAD database files between systems manufactured by different companies.

INTELLIGENT SCANNER: Scanner has additional capabilities such as the ability to recognize characters (OCR) automatically.

INTERLEAVING: The process of breaking up and reordering blocks of data to cause a long error burst to be turned, after de-interleaving, into many short bursts, each of which can be corrected by the error correcting code in use.

J

JUKEBOX: Automatic media handlers for optical disk drives; Also called libraries. Jukeboxes may support multiple disks online at any one time with offline disks quickly accessed mechnically using a robotic arm.

K

KERR EFFECT: Certain substances, when exposed to a magnetic field, will rotate the plane of polarization of light reflected from them. This phase change is called the Kerr effect.

L

LATENCY: The component of the delay in access to data which comes from waiting for a disk to rotate to the desired azimuth. Average latency for a disk drive is usually one-half the rotational period.

LBA: Logical Block Address is the number used to locate a particular block of data on a disk drive.

M

MAGNETO-OPTICAL: A relatively new optical storage technology which combines laser and magnetic methods to read and write from a platter. Information stored by local magnetization of a magnetic medium, using a focused light beam to produce local heating and consequent reduction of coercivity so that a moderately strong, poorly localized magnetic field can flip the state of a small region of high-coercivity material. Reading is done either magnetically, with inductive heads in close proximity to the medium, or optically, through rotation of the plane of polarization of probing light via the Faraday effect or Kerr effect.

MCLV (Modified Constant Linear Velocity): In MCLV, the tracks are divided into bands. Within a band, the disk spins at a constant angular velocity, but that velocity is different for each band. The relation between velocity and band location is similar to the velocity versus radius curve for CLV operation.

MOUNT: An operation which makes the contents of a volume available to a file system.

O

OCR: Abbreviation for Optical Character Recognition. A process of recognizing characters or numbers in printed form through the use of photoelectric technology. Also called optical scanning.

OPTICAL HEAD: An assembly within an optical drive containing the com ponents that reflect laser light on the data surface of the disc and convert the reflected light into electrical signals that can be interpreted as data. Components in the optical head are the laser, lenses, prisms, a focusing mechanism and a photodetector.

P

PEL: Corresponds to pixel. Describes the raster density in terms of black/white characters or images such as pel/cm or pel/in.

PIXEL: Picture element.

R

RASTER: Normal mode of scanning a page from right to left and top to bottom. Image pixels are normally written on a display monitor in raster format.

RECORD HANDLE: A number used to locate a particular record on an optical disk. Analogous to LBA, but composed of two components:

a sector number and a record number within the sector.

S

SECTOR: A triangular section of a disk surface. A block of data is addressed by its track and sector numbers.

SEEK ERROR: The drive's laser is unable to accurately locate user requested data as a result of physical and/or mechanical problems such as vibration, disc surface irregularities, and poor laser focusing.

SEEK TIME: The time required to make as storage unit ready to access a specific location by selection or physical positioning. In optical disk technology, the time required to position the optical read/write head to the desired track.

SMALL COMPUTER SYSTEM INTERFACE (SCSI): A standard 8-bit par allel interface frequently used to connect computer disk drives to a microcomputer. SCSI provides a logical, rather than a physical command set.

SYNC: An operation which brings all files and directories on a volume up to date.

T

TEMPLATE: Stylized character pattern in computer code form that is matched against scanned pixel data to recognize a letter or number.

THINNING: Algorithm to derive the center line of the pixel pattern of a line or mark for accurate representation of the original drawing.

THRESHOLDING: The process by which analog gradation of dark to light is recognized by the scanner's detection mechanism to produce digital signals.

THROUGHPUT: Time required to convert hardcopy to a usage file (ASCII or vector) in a scanning system.

TRANSFER RATE: The rate at which data is transferred to or from a device, especially the reading or writing rate of a storage peripheral. Usually expressed in kilobits or megabits per second.

U

UNMOUNT: An operation which makes the contents of a volume unavailable to a file system. In the ODFS, this operation includes a Sync operation.

V

VECTOR DATA: Converted digital image raster data: formatted data describes spatial locations and geometric relationships of image objects, symbols, and features. Used primarily in CAD/CAM/CAE systems.

VECTORIZATION: Post process of a scanner system when alphanumeric characters, lines, drawings or sketches are converted from raster code to vectors.

VOLUME: One unit of removable storage. The contents of one optical disk surface.

W

WORM (Write-Once, Read-Many):acronym for a Write-Once optical medium which allows the user to write data once (permanently onto the medium) and to read data stored on the medium indefinitely.

References

Berg, B.A. and Roth, J.P. *Software for Optical Storage.* Westport, CT: Meckler Publishing, 1989.

Helgerson, L W. *Introduction to Scanning* Silver Spring, MD: Association for Information and Image Management, 1987.

Parker, S. P. (Ed.). *McGraw Hill Dictionary of Computers,* New York, NY: McGraw-Hill, 1984.

Ralston, A. (Ed.) *Encyclopedia of Computer Science* (first edition). New York: Van Nostrand Reinhold Co., 1976.

Rothchild, E. *Glossary of Optical Memory Terms.* San Francisco, CA: Rothchild Consultants, 1985.

Walsh, M, E. *Understanding Computers: What Managers and Users Need to Know.* New York: John Wiley & Sons, Inc., 1981.

Wetzler, F. U. *Desktop Image Scanners and Scanning.* Silver Spring, MD: Association for Information and Image Management, 1989.

Contributors

Brian A. Berg, president of Berg Software Design, has been in the software industry since 1974, and has been a consultant since 1979. He has implemented device drivers and real-time software under Unix, MS-DOS, MTOS, VMS and AOS. Since 1985, he has implemented a number of systems which use WORM and CD-ROM optical storage and the SCSI interface. His consulting activities have been with firms including Arix (Arete Systems) Corporation, Plexus Computers, Inc., TAB Products Company, Raytel Systems Corporation, E-mu Systems, Inc. TRW (Teknekron) Financial Systems, Acctex Information Systems (IMTECH), and Sequent Computer Systems. He is a contributing editor of *Optical Information Systems* journal and an active participant in Optical Information System conferences in the U.S. and UK. He participates in and helps organize the IEEE Asilomar Microcomputer Workshop held annually near Monterey, CA. He is editor of *Software for Optical Storage* with J.P. Roth (Meckler, 1989) and has published articles in *Systems Integration* and *Optical Information Systems.* He has a B.S. in mathematics from Pacific Lutheran University and attended computer science graduate classes at Stanford University.

Otmar Foelsche is Manager of the Dartmouth College Language Resource Center. A teacher of German, he has taught at the Goethe Institute, the University of Maine, the University of Rhode Island and at Dartmouth College. Other activities include coordinating ESL (English-as-a-Second Language) programs and training teachers and tutors in ESL and foreign languages for the State of Maine. He belongs to a loosely defined group at Dartmouth College called Hyperteam which has traveled abroad as well as to many U.S. institutions presenting Hypercard applications and training. Dr. Foelsche is actively involved in the research and development of the Language Workstation Project, a joint undertaking with Harvard and Brown University.

Joan Sustik Huntley is Research and Development Project Leader, Weeg Computing Center, University of Iowa. She directs the Computer-Assisted Instruction (CAI) Laboratory which conducts research and development on the application of new computing technologies in higher education. Since 1978, much of the Laboratory's work has focused on multimedia applications using a variety of development and delivery configurations including videodisc, WORM and rewritable optical drives on IBM-PC, Macintosh and the NeXT Computer. She received her doctorate in Instructional Design from the University of Iowa in 1978.

Robert B. Mueller, Vice President and General Manager, Rewritable Optical Products Division, Sony Corporation of America has been with the firm for over twenty years. He is responsible for the business development, sales, distribution and support of Sony's rewritable optical disk drives, controllers, and media to OEMs, VARs, systems integrators and large corporate end-users. The Sony Rewritable Optical Products Division is part of the Sony Optical Storage Systems Company and is responsible for the marketing, sales, service and support of Sony's rewritable optical products for the computer industry. Prior to his current position, Mr. Mueller served as vice president of new business development for the Sony Image Products Company and served in executive capacities in Sony's professional video business. He is on the board of Governors of the International Communications Industry Association, and is a member of the National Academy of Television Arts and Sciences, International Television Association, and International Tape Association.

Mary Ann O'Connor is Marketing Manager of Reference Technology, Inc. Prior to her current position, she was President of Compact Discoveries, Inc., a computer applications development firm specializing in optical disk technology. She has been involved in the design of several write-once optical disk-based systems for information storage and retrieval as well as a number of read-only optical disk application products. In addition, she has served as editor, Compact Disc Technologies, *Optical Information Systems Update* and was a contributor to *CD-ROM: The New Papyrus* from Microsoft Corporation, and *CD-ROM Applications and Markets* from Meckler Publishing Corporation, and has written for a variety of other publications.

Michael Partridge is a Programmer for the University of Iowa's Computer-Assisted Instruction Laboratory. He has over seven years of experience in professional positions in data processing at the University of Iowa Hygienic

Laboratory and the University of Iowa Foundation. He has a B.A. in Psychology from the University of Iowa and senior standing in the Department of Computer Science. His interests are in human/computer interactivity, artificial intelligence, and interactive multimedia.

Judith Paris Roth has been involved with optical storage technology since 1979. She is editor-in-chief of *Optical Information Systems* magazine, co-editor-in-chief of *Multimedia Review*, and chairperson of the Annual OIS Conference and Exposition sponsored by Meckler Corporation. She is author of *Essential Guide to CD-ROM*, *CD-ROM Applications and Markets*, *Case Studies of Optical Storage Applications*, and *Converting Information to WORM Optical Storage: A Case Study Approach*. In addition, she is also co-editor of *Software for Optical Storage* with Brian A. Berg. She has written extensively about optical storage technology in *Popular Computing*, *Journal of the American Society of Information Science*, *Library Software Review*, *AAP Newsletter*, *High Technology*, and *Educational and Instructional Television*. She has an M.S.L.S. from Syracuse University and attended the Information Systems Seminar at the Sloan School of Management at the Massachusetts Institute of Technology in 1981.

Geoffrey A. Russell is President of Cascade Materials Research and Development (Beaverton, OR) which provides materials analysis, formulation and consulting services to the radiation curing and optical storage industries. After working on the technical staff of Exxon Research and Engineering and the Eastman Kodak Research Laboratories, he joined Optical Data, Inc. as an Advisory Scientist. He received his B.S. and M.S. degrees in chemical engineering from Massachusetts Institute of Technology and his Ph.D. in material science and engineering from the University of Utah.

Index